FINISH IT

FINISH IT

MEMOIR OF FINDING MY MUSIC, MY TRUTH, AND MY TRUE LOVE

By Dorian Marie

MILL CITY PRESS

Mill City Press, Inc.
2301 Lucien Way #415
Maitland, FL 32751
407.339.4217
www.millcitypress.net

© 2019 by Dorian Marie
Finish It
Memoir of Finding My Music, My Truth, and My True Love

All rights reserved solely by the author. The author guarantees all contents are original and do not infringe upon the legal rights of any other person or work. No part of this book may be reproduced in any form without the permission of the author. The views expressed in this book are not necessarily those of the publisher.

Printed in the United States of America.

ISBN-13: 978-1-5456-7291-4

TABLE OF CONTENTS

Beginning or End? 1
My New Lifework 19
I Only Said Yes Because He Asked 31
A New Perspective for Me 56
DorianMarie; The Making of 67
My Love Life 78
15 Minutes 97
My Issues With Love 99
More on the Love Front 111
Fox & I Learned the Hard Way 117
Will They Return? 121
My Lifelines 126
Lessons Learned 131
It's Almost Time 137
The Album 143

BEGINNING OR END?

The last thing I heard, or shall I say read from him, was a text that said, "I'm done with you" in 2012; Devastated. The last thing I heard from my church was "Silence" in 2013; Shocked. The last thing I heard from God was, "Take it all down, the music, the book, social media, the website..." in 2015; Angry! Simultaneously, I felt rejected by the three most precious and sacred aspects of my whole existence. And how ironic for it to happen in 2015, exactly 20 years from the start of it all. I began my journey in love, music, and faith in 1995 (although there was what I thought to be my "first love" at the age of 13). I find it remarkable that it was only when these three areas fell apart that I felt peace with rejection. It was supposed to happen that way. The 20-year journey of *Dorian* as everyone had known her to be or even as I had known myself to be, was complete. I realized that during those 20 years, my relationships, church, and music always intertwined. In 2015, I laid it all down, walked away, confused, hurt, and lost but at peace. Disclaimer: This book is not about my religious beliefs or God, but about my journey, which includes an in-depth life of years in religion, which is an intricate part of my past. Therefore, I'll refer to it often, mostly at the beginning of the book.

So how do I explain a three-year sabbatical from social media or going off the grid so to speak, and a 2018 social media come back dressed in a wife beater singing love songs?

New Path

It was about finding the truth. *My* truth. The truth about my faith, my music, and true love. I needed to find out what I truly believed about these three aspects of my life not based on what someone told me, society, religion, the culture, or tradition. But what was I going to be at peace believing? Right or wrong, finding and reconciling my truth was between myself and God so that this time around, my convictions would align with the authentic me. Sure, it is scary and unsettling to dig up your foundations to revisit what lies underneath and ponder if you still hold those beliefs and why. But it's even more frightening to look back over your life and see that you lived someone else's who has gone on with theirs in a whole different direction. Now part of this book is for previous supporters who have followed my journey three years ago and over the last 20 years. I'm sure you expected a different type of album. The other part of this book is for my new connections, friends, and supporters.

Girl, Where Have You Been?

Honestly, I had no plans for a return. I was content. In these three years, I built my *first* dream house and bought two brand new cars, both in my name only, went back and finished college and received my bachelor's degree in Counseling. I went on to earn my master's degree (both degrees between the age of 35-37) in Education Administration, became a health teacher, obtained a few more certifications and became my dad's Power of Attorney for health reasons. This all while raising my kids as a single mother and focusing on my coins. Significant accomplishments considering, well, my life. I'm creating an inheritance for my kids, leaving a legacy of wealth and grit. Show them how to finish it! Yep. I began all these endeavors at the age of 18, but life happened paired with my choices. I had to re-start again as a grown adult, but I am about to finish it with this album, new book and indeed a new love partnership. To my surprise, I am just getting started again in this new cycle of my life.

Now hear this, I say my truth as I am still growing, evolving and changing and it's vital that we allow people to stand in their truth with no judgment. I want to emphasize the word *allow*. Allow people to be who they are. As of today, I am the most authentic version of myself. I thought I was authentic before I got involved with church, music, and love. But that is not true. I remember being in the 5th grade, trying to wear my hair like my Caucasian or Hispanic counterparts in school. I noticed that my ponytail didn't move like theirs. And when they wore leggings with the lace around the bottom, mine filled out a little bit more at the top than theirs at the hip and buttocks. So, I ran circles around my house every day after school, trying to lose weight as a 10-year-old, to get rid of my curves. From that time on, that is how I lived; trying to be someone else or settling with an "I'm just not good enough" mentality.

This three-year journey was about me becoming and accepting my true authentic self, right or wrong. I know my truth and walk freely in it. But, is it about being right or wrong? Because what is right or wrong for me is not the same for the next person. Yes, some moral truths and laws apply to all humanity for our safety and well-being, but when it comes to my liberties and my path, it's about peace with my Creator and myself. I remember meditating about this transition and the type of music I was now drawn to sing, as opposed to singing about God primarily as I did in the past. I also recall the response to that prayer. "You are singing about God because He is love. Sing about love. Sing music that heals."

My Journal Entries

This book idea came from my music dad and manager, Jim Finley, whom during a much-needed father-daughter pow- wow, said that I needed to write my story, starting with where I've been, where I am now until I finish the album and present them to the world together. I am one that journals, so that was perfect for me. And I've written a book before entitled, *Let's Talk it Out*. It bears mentioning because his reasoning's made so much sense. I wrote my first book from a different perspective in my faith than where I am now as well as being a different person then. It's a faith-based book, and I've since then changed a few of my beliefs. This current book is a memoir. It fills in the gap regarding my transition musically and spiritually and answers frequent questions I am receiving from past and present supporters about my music and life's journey. Mainly, "Where have you been?" and "What kind of music are you singing now?"

As part of this memoir, you will get to read my journal entries in real time as I'm writing this book. Cool, huh? You know what else? The cover of the actual journal that I was writing in this whole time, says, *Write Your Story* on the front, given to me by my friend right before I started this journey. I only noticed it after my conversation with my music dad. Synchronistic for sure. Thanks, Jim!

CHANGE HAS COME

August 2018

Let me fast forward then backtrack. On 12/18/18, a co-worker said he was following me on social media in awe that I was singing somewhere almost every weekend and wanted to know what sparked this sudden blast of appearances, photo shoots, book signings, and events. What made me start doing this again? Here is where it began.

It is the first week of August. I was minding my own business, enjoying my three years away from the world, when an acquaintance decides to visit unexpectedly. His friend passed away a few days prior in an accident. I wasn't on any social media at that time and was gearing up to start my 3rd year as a health teacher. There wasn't a tune in my thoughts, a song in my spirit or a melody in my heart. Mind you. I hadn't touched a keyboard in five years or sung in public outside of my uncle's homegoing/funeral service in June 2017, and then my aunt's service that same year in December.

Those were the only two public events since 2013, and my keyboard had been in storage for the last five years as well. In 2017, when I moved into my new house after living with my mom for those five years to take care of my father, I set up the keyboard in an empty spare room and never touched it. I just looked at it in passing for the two years I've been living here until he came over.

He starts telling me about what happened to his friend. His friend was a great father, husband, and leader, and well respected in his circle of influence. His words softened my heart to do the video tribute when he asked. We went to the room where my dusty keyboard was and started singing and playing around on the keys. I was asked to sing *A Change is Gonna Come* by Sam Cooke. In my head, I thought, "Um sir, I know of the song and the first few lyrics from movies and such, but I've only sung and played gospel, and even that was five years ago." I had never played that one. He kept pushing, pushing, and pushing me to play and sing it, and he sang a verse too. I sat down at the keyboard, sung and played the song for the first time by ear with the lyrics pulled up on my phone.

We played with the song for two hours to perfect it as best we could. I don't know about him, but your girl was struggling. My estranged vocal cords were wide-eyed and perplexed I'm sure, just as I was, and confused. Although he is not a singer, he enjoys singing. I didn't anymore. He kept saying how much fun he was having, but it wasn't fun for me, at all. He made the video and posted it...on his Facebook! I figured he would show some of his friends and members of the family as his tribute since he claims he cannot sing. But social media? I was low key irritated at first but

FINISH IT

let it go because it blessed many people. But I wasn't ready for the questions about my disappearing act, with whom or where I was singing now or who might recognize me. And I couldn't see what was happening because I deleted all my social media platforms.

The Next Day

He sent me a screenshot of the views as if that was a consolation. I was irritated, and I made sure he knew it. But because the response was so positive, I too showed only my friends and family via text. They were shocked that I was singing again! And because they all knew that Dorian didn't fool with men/love anymore, I also understood the, "You have a *MAN* in the video?!" replies. More on that question later. But this fella sends me a screenshot the next day of over 1,000 views from his page and casually says, "Oh yeah, I put it on my YouTube page too." I was livid! He did what?! Put it on YouTube?! I wasn't happy at all. I asked him if he was ready for this kind of attention, critique, and feedback. I was not! I wanted to stay comfortable and away from it all. Why did he do that? Sigh. It took me days to process this and even more so, I was upset because I looked the hottest of all messes as he decided to show up at my house spontaneously! I barely had time to fix my hair and put on my face. I was mad, for real. But the thought of someone losing a loved one shadowed my frustration, and I could only imagine what the family was going through. I sing at funerals all the time, and it was an honor if not in person to be able to sing on behalf of his friend.

The Next Phase

Well, a few days passed, and he demands that I sing various covers to put on his page. WHY?! His behavior went on like this for a few weeks. I ended up covering a few songs, and he posted them. Something started to wake up in me. What in the world was happening? During this time, my daughter and I received some rather tough news, and we were down about it. It was the second week of August, and he hits me up about doing a cover on that Saturday. Our hearts were hurting from days of dealing with this news. I must say it was a great idea and a distraction. We started recording and playing around with different songs, and it took our minds off the issue. It was an all-day adventure of laughing and singing with my daughter and then she turned into him. Directing me to sing this and sing it this way, or nope do it over. It was chaotic fun. We recorded it and sent it to him. You think a person is in your life for one reason and then you see it is for another. His purpose was to open me back up to music, and for that, I am grateful.

We Had A Deal

For the rest of August, I went into hermit mode, solitude. "God, are You kidding me? We had a deal! No more music! What are You doing...saying?" Also, at this time my heart was broken over the news given to me and the kids, on top of the fact that someone I sincerely cared about didn't feel the same about me or failed to express it. Although I would hear and watch him express feelings to other people. I will get more into my love life later. Just nosey (smile). So, I am supposed to start singing songs and posting them? Where? I have no following anymore, no more social media pages, no platform, nothing. Finally, I got a grip.

Oh, as of 08/21/18, I am officially dating, like for real! There hasn't been anything substantial on the dating end since 2010. There was one guy I saw for about two years. Well, I was seeing him, but he was not seeing me if you know what I mean. You will have to wait for the love section of this book for the details. But I am excited and lost at the same time.

WHAT IS HAPPENING?

September 2018

At this point, I'm not sure what the Universe has in mind. I started writing songs when I was 15 years old — songs about love, encouraging people, and my love for God primarily. Now, I'm dealing with a lot of pain from the present, and I'm sure from the past. What is the solution? Write about it. Now I see what's happening. I've lost some connections over the last two years that shocked me, and I'm going to process this pain through songs. Gotcha. "Wait, did You say on an album too? Are You kidding me? ...Again?!?!" My punctuation is not an exaggeration, and my talks with the Creator were at an all-time high at this point. Once you read my story, you will understand better. I killed and buried that album dream! As well as the idea of having a partner. Anxiety is starting to set in alongside the confusion. Anyway, back to the person I cared about who acted like we were on the same page. I wrote a song about it. Later in the book, I will explain each song. The songs are about my relationships and connections over the last two years.

So, here's the plan. I'm going to sing songs about life, friendships, relationships and such. I'm going to write about my evolution, growth, and changes in my mindset that I have experienced since I left the grid. Okay.

A New Thing

Deciding to walk in my new-found truth, of course, I knew there would be questions, concerns, furrowed brows, prayers about and for me, and maybe even confusion. I don't blame anyone because I felt the same way. I heard the conversations and thoughts: "She left us as the worship leader, Christian author, minister, and speaker and came back as...?" I returned as Dorian, the one I was always and eventually meant to be. I like her a lot, and on September 23, 2018, I blurted the words, "I love you, girl!" to myself as I was walking around my house. Out of nowhere. You may not believe this, but this was the first time I have ever said those words to myself, and it bled out naturally. But now the task at hand was to present the *real* Dorian which would be foreign to most. And this time it didn't matter who loved me or not or if they agreed with me or not. Because I have discovered self-love. Finally.

There was also the task of figuring out how to explain in minimal characters, often in my DM's or online, "What kind of artist are you?" which one gentleman asked sincerely after reviewing an array of various genre covers, I posted on Facebook. I was navigating this new season in my life, as well as bringing clarity with compassion to others who were not so sincere. At times people silently and openly judged what they could not understand. I sympathize as I have done it too.

9/18/18 "Ras" (Lil Raskull), and I chopped it up about what I was going to be doing musically this time around. It was different and not what people would expect. And he spoke words of rest to me when he said, "What you want to do, it is legal." Still processing that.

9/19/18 Music dad charged me up today as I mentioned earlier with a weighty conversation that grounded me musically and energetically. He gave me a focus that I desperately needed.

Running from Jim

I wanted to make a move musically, and I knew deep down he would disagree, or shall I say steer me in a different direction. Peace was lacking as I dealt with the feeling that I might be getting ahead of myself if I make this move. Sooo, for days, I ran from him and planned on just doing it, and he would see it online after

FINISH IT

the fact. I tried talking to someone else who I knew would agree to make me feel better, but they referred me back to him. *Irritating*. When I finally spoke to Jim, he informed me that he felt like we needed to connect the whole day I was energetically running from him. He sensed it. I sent him a long justifying text about what and why I wanted to take this action. And it is something all artist want to do but should wait, or they could regret it. He replied with a stern direct text, followed up with smiley faces and a request to call him. (Me: Lip smacking and a little rolling of the eyes). See, I knew he would say no! But he gave me a proper perspective and wisdom from the heavens. It was a breakthrough moment that set the tone for this book, this album and the discipline I needed to write, write, and write. Thank you, Jim.

These two conversations were the catalyst to even more personal growth and precision in the next steps that I would take.

I must mention my use of the word *Universe* before people label me as being "new age". Have I expanded my thinking? Yes, but I take terms and use them in ways that resonate with me. I believe that God does not work alone, although He can. We are co-creators with Him. He uses angels, His Spirit, us, signs on the street, music, a message on a shirt, a donkey or whatever to bring about circumstances in our lives to speak to us if we would only look and listen. He meets us where we are and can communicate through any medium if the intent behind it is pure. Angels lead and guide us to turn on the radio at the right time or walk outside to take out the trash just to run into someone with our answer or to give one (real story). So, this is what I mean by the word *Universe*.

9/23/18 Today, while talking to Ras, he asked me what the name of my album was going to be. I told him that was still undecided, seeing that I have two or three different genres or sounds that I want to put out at once. And it is not "Christian" music as people would expect. Feeling blocked. I have this genre, then this sound, and then a whole other genre, but it's all me! He said I

BEGINNING OR END?

think you just named your album. Me: Huh? Ras: My Other Playlist. Does that not sum up my message, journey, and future course? Thanks, Ras!

When it comes to the title of the album, I must backtrack here remembering a conversation that occurred on 09/16/2018 when I first met up with my friend Julius Anderson who produced the *"Overjoyed"* cover I did. I shared the plan with him and where I was going musically. I remember him lightheartedly commenting and saying, "So Christians can have other playlists'?" I didn't catch it then. So thankful how things can come around again (while talking to Ras) like when you miss it the first time. And I realized we had this conversation the day we did the cover on 10/19/2018. Thanks, Julius!

MY OTHER PLAYLIST

Here is a perfect place to explain the album, *My Other Playlist*. Directly and indirectly, as a kid, the church taught that one should only engage with Gospel/Christian music, movies, Christian events, etc. To do so, was a form of protection against the wiles of the devil and the ways of the world so that one does not end up in hell. But I find this way of thinking to be fear based to an extent and legalistic, and this is how I lived my Christian life growing up. Afraid. Now part of my legalistic ways can be credited to my personality type. When I do something, I go all in. I may have taken things to the extreme. I think I used to pray over my gum. At least that is what my cousin told me, and I believe her.

My Other Playlist is not a faith-based album. During my 3-year awakening as I would call it that began in 2015 up until now, my mind and heart have expanded in the way I express my faith and spiritual life. I have accepted what my mind and heart were trying to tell me since I was 15-years old. 1995, was the year Selena Quintanilla-Perez died. She was and still is one of my favorite

FINISH IT

singers. My insecurity also attracted me to her. See, I attempted modeling around this age, and the agency informed me that I was too short and curvy. As I looked around at the other girls, not only was I the only dark spot in the room but the only one with meat on her bones. I was out of place for sure. So, whenever I saw Selena on stage, I thought if people could accept her figure, then maybe I'd be okay too. You didn't see a lot of people that looked like Selena at the forefront. I would sneak and listen to her music. I didn't even speak Spanish, but it's the reason I translated my Christian music into Spanish and eventually my current music. I was known as the black girl that sang like a white girl but sang in Spanish. A Christian influenced by Selena? I was conflicted but hid it. This stifling had a snowball effect on every part of my life. I lived a sheltered life due to religious conditioning and fear of damnation for over 20 years.

I Like That Non-Gospel Song, and I'm Not Going to Hell for It

2017 exposed me to new things and new people that were strategically placed in my life to break me out of self-imprisonment and bondage. New music for sure! I am embracing my liberties, preferences, and have transformed into a being that I genuinely enjoy. The album title represents my truth that I don't have to sing songs that speak about God's attributes for them to be considered from or of Him or to be considered acceptable. I have other playlists/songs that promote love, forgiveness, justice, or a dance-off with my daughter (which happened), and they were not from Christian artists. I remember the judgment I felt for wanting to pat my feet to the song, *Happy* by Pharrell. I pretended like I didn't like it, but my soul was crying to get "Happy"! My mom and aunt loved that song, and I used to give them that religious side-eye when it came on as they would dance around the living room. I was crazy. My argument was, yes it may be an okay song, but he also sings those "other type" of songs, correct? That is just one example. More on this later.

9/25/18 I posted a country song, and it was a cover of one of my favorite songs by Brett Young. In response to this video, a stranger by the name of Jim Clark messaged me and said, "Dorian, you are a Worshipper...this is very true regardless of what you sing. Once a mantle is placed on you, you are extremely penetrating regardless of any genre of music. Anointed music transcends beyond the walls of the church into a world of hurting, hopeless, and searching people."

Man, this set me straight! No need to expound. J. Clark has no clue that earlier that day, my mind was seeking validation for what I was doing, and he was my confirmation. I don't even solicit comments or critique from anyone. I just posted it, and he in-boxed that message like an angel in disguise. I will say, that I did think it strange at first him connecting a country song to the essence of who I am, one who heals through music. But he was an angel with a message, a stranger who I entertained. I struggled at the start of this journey in October with the music that I desired to sing. Words like this are God winks to me, which I get even more now along this journey.

9/26/18 I miss him. I'm not even sure who he is, but I miss him. I wish he were here before it all happens to ease my suspicions of him coming to ride the glory. A few have done that recently. Dorian, your ease comes from knowing that you are not going to attract that again because you don't resonate with that type of energy. Change your thoughts, girl.

9/27/18 I ran across Russell White's cover of *Better Days*. Much needed as I consider how in the world will I get all this done, the book, the album, the photo shoots, the music video??? As a single mother, I am fully trusting that the provision will be present for this vision.

Venting

Do you know what can be frustrating in this process? When people come to you with a gamut or catalog of music ideas of what you should do or better yet what you *should* have done by now. If they only knew what I have been through and the priorities I have placed above my dreams. I appreciate the dialogue, but I would appreciate their funds with that dialogue. That adds stress when a person comes to you, a single mom, and dumps all these great ideas on you about what you should do and then leaves you to carry the load of how it will get done.

9/27/18 Another, "What kind of artist are you?" in my inbox. Every time this is asked, my answer becomes more defined. I spent an hour on the phone sharing and connecting with this person. It was nice. A stranger on Facebook, and musician at a well-known church, and very open to what I am striving to do.

What Kind of Artist Are You, Again?

Here is another way for me to answer the question about the switch from singing Christian music to all music. Nothing has changed, but the objective of my songs. When I was singing strictly Christian music, I wrote and sang songs that related to my love for God. Now I sing about the love between people or the love in human relationships. People will assume that I have turned away from God or as they say, have backslidden. The truth is, we are humans no matter what our faith is. And as humans, we experience things in friendships and relationships. As a songwriter, I write songs, even if they are not related to faith. All I am doing now is writing songs about my human relationships just like I used to write and sing songs about my relationship with Him. I forgot that I did and still do sing for weddings. So, my Christian music career was sprinkled with loves songs now and then. And it is highly possible that I will continue to write faith-based songs and release them as well, even if other artists sing them. I still have several in my repertoire.

Second Time Around

As far as working with Jim, this is not our first rodeo together. After two failed album launches, I decided to get back in the saddle in 2013. I wrote this song called *Let Me Be*. I wrote the lyrics and basic melody, but Jim and another producer, M.M., produced the track and all the fancy stuff. Now, I see the process of making that type of song was a precursor of what I am doing today. First, they are white guys. I am colored. That wasn't the issue because I was labeled a white girl all my life; "You need some more soul in your voice and music." So, I went to churches that sung Contemporary Christian music like Hillsong and Kari Jobe. That fit me, and so did these two producers.

With this song, these guys were taking me out of my comfort zone. Not because it wasn't me, but what would the people say? What would the church say since it is not about worshiping God and His attributes? Who are these two white guys? And, we recorded it in the same studio that Chris Brown recorded in and many other non-gospel artists. That is a no-no, but I didn't care. It was a Christian song, yes, but it was about my personal life and frustrations about the setbacks in music and failed relationships.

It was new to me, and every part of me wanted to do this song and was so proud of it. When I got home from L.A., and we released it, the struggle was real. Why am I letting these people put me in a box? Jim knew that I could not, nor was I ready to fully embrace it. The real me that wanted to be and do something different was not prepared for what the Universe was trying to get me to do. But I am ready now.

I never told him this, but M.M. is the one that gave me the confidence to record and play my chords/music in the studio. Playing live, yes. Studio, no. I was terrified and insecure, so he did it for me.

This time around when Jim told me to play the chords, I felt a little annoyed at first, but immediately saw in my head how M.M. positioned his hands with confidence and played those chords back then. And he primarily plays the guitar, bass, etc., like a beast! So, if he could do it, I can do it. And I did. Thanks, guy.

Balance

People may and have assumed that I have no faith or have denied mine, but this new path calls for me to be even more spiritually grounded, not religious, but spiritually grounded because my audience is not just the church but humanity. As you have seen on social media, people are quick to put their mouth on you, drag you, and give commentary on just about everything you do when you are in the limelight. One needs to be spiritually grounded to withstand it all. I have and will continue to embrace balance in every area of my life, especially with music. Will I ever record Christian music again? I am open to anything that resonates with my soul and brings light to humanity.

GETTING COMFORTABLE

October 2018

I am starting to settle in little by little in this new genre and the idea of singing love music or just music for the world. I am embracing the side of me that loves people, a love partner, my children, and myself.

BEGINNING OR END?

10/03/18 I met up with my friend D.D. for tea. I never get tired of talking and listening to this guy. It's like everything he says makes you think. It's been three years since we last met for one of our "intellectual meals" and I shared with him where I was now with my music and my life. He referred me to a song by Donnie Hathaway entitled *I Believe in Music*. Boy, I tell you. When I went to listen to the song in the car, it was as if D.D. was telling me, "Dorian, I was listening to you today." Love and music.

10/6/18 Wow. A Facebook message from a family member of the "I'm done with you" guy I spoke of at the start of this book! I am not surprised. On your healing journey and before you go into the next season of your life, things will come up and return for final healing or clearing, to see if you have completely forgiven, evaluate where you stand and if you learned the lesson.

Let me tell you, the songs on this album include all my encounters in love, including this one. I finally spoke my truth to his family member. Why? Because I've always covered people, especially if they were/are well known and respected by society. Yes, you cover other people's weaknesses with love, but you do not cover the hurt it caused you. That was my fault all these years, covering people for their comfort while I suffered silently in the "name of Christ". I explained to his family member what he did and how it made me feel, and that I'd forgiven him. I wrote a song about it. More on that later. It was the first time I acknowledged what he did to me openly.

10/7/18 My cousin Timothy messaged me: "I have always loved your music. Can't wait to see what becomes of the journey you are on and how it will come to fruition." Yep. That got me. Tissue, please.

His wife Elena *always* has an encouraging word, and it's right on time! Such a beautiful family.

FINISH IT

10/8/18 Inbox message: "What kind of music do you do?" Me: Music that inspires and promotes love. That is the shortest response thus far. I say shortest because my lifework is defined through this journey, day by day.

10/8/18 I wonder if love will find me by the time this book and album is complete or just anytime soon? I miss him. Whoever "him" is. Or maybe this feeling is him missing me? Well, I know you are out there. We will meet soon. I feel you.

Regarding the three sacred aspects of my life that I spoke of, I will say that I am still waiting for love as I cultivate my faith and music. One of my challenges in this process is developing my real voice and changing my tone from a "churchy sound" where you could sing anyway you want for the most part and get away with pretty much anything vocally. You would get feedback such as, "That's alright baby, just sing for the Lord" if you messed up a run or note. Back then, the church was generous. Today, social media is ruthless, and you will become a meme! Now I have an intentional sound. And that's not to say that while singing in the church that I put no effort into my craft.

On the contrary, I perfected my voice for the sound of that season in my life. But now I have the task of developing my sound for this season.

MY NEW LIFEWORK

When it comes to music, I am here to invest in all types of relationships through music, writing, and speaking. One aspect of my lifework is to provide music that you can sing to with your friend or lover. It makes sense seeing that a real love relationship is all I have ever wanted as many people do. I have learned that most times, it's not that we are terrible, lousy people that things do not work out. But we have both been through things that we still need to heal. Sometimes we put ourselves in those positions or toxic connections when a time of solitude and healing is required instead. Other times, people come in and trigger our healing. When you're alone, sometimes you cannot see the necessary inner work within that still needs to be done. Someone else will come in as your mirror and vice versa, to reveal to each other what unfinished business lies underneath.

If you are wondering why you keep attracting the same kind of person, and it ends up in disaster or ends abruptly, consider taking time alone. Go within, clear out old patterns, heal, become a better version of yourself, and you will be surprised by the results and how you will attract a better fit for you.

10/7/18 Daily now it seems like it is just me and you keyboard. I remember during this three-year music drought that I could not stand to see you. I would walk past your room, roll my eyes, or act as if you didn't exist. And five years before that you were in storage. But I kept you. I never touched you, but I kept you. You reminded me of love deferred, faith that failed, and dreams unfulfilled. But I kept you.

10/10/18 I am still in hermit mode as I transform into more of me. Very encouraged by my music dad and my vocal mechanic. These guys are heaven sent! They do not know each other but spoke the same things to me within hours of each other. I had questions, and they had answers. Some of those answers: I am secure as a Christian/Gospel singer but insecure about just being a singer. The singer I authentically am. My coach exposed my comfort zones as far as key-signatures, choice of voice, and go-to habits.

10/12/18 Last night, I was in such a beautiful space and energy. I felt His presence and *his* presence. I am sitting here writing this book and playing a mix of songs in the background. All the songs were slow, spiritual or romantic and what I wanted and needed to hear without me even saying it. Every time I fell asleep and woke up, a new song would begin, and it resonated with the space I was in at the moment. Intimate. I felt like I was close to God and with him, and no sex was involved. And he is not even in my life at this point whoever he is. I felt them both, and it was so sweet and encouraging.

10/12/18 As I watch different people singing on YouTube and doing covers such as myself and listening to various artists, I realize that unique people are untouchable or unstoppable. My friend Julius made this comment when he sent me the cover by *Esperanza Spalding* for us to work on. He said that she was untouchable. And rightfully so! She is her authentic self. People will always compare, but it's hard to compare someone when they are their unique self. It is when we try to be like other people that we put ourselves in a category to be compared. I like to say *know your package*. Esperanza knows her package. She can stand up with her bass instrument and sing. I cannot. Every artist has a package they present to the world, and when we know it and embrace it, we are untouchable! As an artist, staying in your lane

MY NEW LIFEWORK

keeps you in a league of your own, with no room to compare or compete or a need to.

10/16/18 Well the *Overjoyed* cover is done. It was supposed to be a simple-dimple-easy peasy-task. But nope. Julius being Julius. I didn't come dressed for that nor did he TELL me in advance, that I would be on camera. Such a plotter. But it worked out great, and it was super fun! It was the first time in five years that I had been in front of a studio mic. I made a pact with myself to never go back to the studio, but here I was.

WHOA, this just happened!

At the end of this book, I will explain the lyrics to the songs you hear on the album. In *Love For You*, I mention three people who just fell off this year, one of them last year. Well, on 10/21/18, two of which I refer to in the first verse both hit me up on the same day! I was "shooketh"! But at the same time, at peace, because there was a need for *allowing* as I mentioned before. These were not just casual connections. I am talking about family and intimate relationships. Intimacy does not always mean sex guys. Geez. Anyway, in speaking to one of them, we realized that it was necessary. It had been five months, and one day the calls, texts, and visits just stopped. On a soul level, I wanted this, needed this. But we get co-dependent on relationships, fear total loss again, or feel obligated even though we know the connection is not where it needs to be. Separation with an understanding can save a relationship. This person spoke about how they wanted to reach out but could not because it wasn't time. I could feel this person at times, and I do believe you can send messages to people telepathically or some would say spiritually. You do it all the time when you "speak over" someone or pray for them. Or you have heard people say, "I felt your prayers."

I am processing it all and still healing. We both are. It hurt. But lessons had to be learned.

10/22/2018 Julius reluctantly calls to inform me that his Mac computer crashed that contained all the vocals and music we did for the cover song. It is okay. Really.

10/23/2018 Julius sends me an email of the finished product. He recovered it. I was *overjoyed* hoping that he didn't have to spend money to fix it.

MY VOCAL MECHANIC

I call my vocal coach a vocal mechanic. "You had a vocal coach? But you can sing already," you say. Yes, I can sing, but I wanted to learn how to sing outside of a one-dimensional sound that I cultivated in the church. Even the top pop singers have vocal coaches. Yes, I know I can sing, but when you are treading new waters, it's good to have a multi-dimensional guide to help you. We only had two sessions together. He brought out of me what was already there for this new sound. Your car will run fine by itself, but it still needs occasional maintenance. People have told me, or they have posted that I cannot sing, and I need this and that. But they do not understand my process or journey. Ignorance, so they get a pass.

First, I have been singing for over 20 years, and I know when I sound like crap, I am flat, or off. But I still would post cover videos with mistakes. Second, there was a bigger purpose behind my covers that were not vocally sound or perfect. You are talking about a person who has not sung, and I mean even in the car or turned the radio on because I was on this anti-music kick for five years. Third, Jim, bless his heart, has witnessed my regimen before I sing as I have suffered from severe year-round allergies and sinus issues. It is not pretty, and I am seeking professional help because I cannot take this anymore. But, no cameras, no stage, no events or reason to practice or use my voice in five years. Then, last year, out of the blue, I turn on the camera, the keyboard, sing a song, record it, and post it.

Even if I did want to hear music, what would I listen to at this point? At the time, I didn't listen to other genres, so I could not listen to secular music. I didn't want to hear Christian music to remind me of what happened in the church, so I listened to nothing. What was amazing to me and those closest to me was that I was singing again period. The type of music didn't matter to them. I posted those covers starting in August to see myself and what it would be like to sing these type of songs as it was out of my comfort zone. I think by the 7th cover song, I was like, okay. Okay.

Here They Come

People have made comments on my cover songs. For the most part, people are generous with their positive comments. At the time I am writing this chapter, I can count on one hand the negative ones I have seen, but that does not account for the ones that people thought but didn't post. For one, I'm not here to perfect cover songs. For me, singing these specific cover songs was strategic and requested by supporters. It wasn't about perfection, but about having fun. Doing it for the sake of "Oh my goodness, I am not singing Gospel, this is different, but I love it" and to be authentic in conveying my feelings through the song. Of course, I should work on focusing on the notes at times when I sing covers or whatever. Every singer does, but at this point in my journey, it was about singing, period. I also give primary attention to the lyrical meaning and emotion behind a song. One day in December, I posted five requested cover songs in one day. I didn't know the lyrics or chords but was familiar with the songs. I did those in one hour, changed clothes so the thumbnails would be different and crammed lyrics and chords in my brain. Pretty impressive to me. And a few select people were worried about an off note?

FINISH IT

Now my album will be perfect as humanly possible because people are not paying to hear mess. With my covers, I am not deaf. But it wasn't wise to spend time perfecting them over perfecting my original songs for the album with my deadline. While recording my records, I send Jim on a search and rescue for off notes, and ask him regularly, if he heard that? Or what was that sound? Let me do that over. People are paying for this, so it matters.

I posted covers for myself, to be honest. And if people felt it, great. But people have never been my audience, especially when singing in the church. Today, my audience is myself first, *then* anyone who gets the overflow of that. It's about how I feel, and the feeling I want to convey and most importantly, the message. Now in relationships, I have been a people pleaser in the past, but never in music. According to some, I sing like a white girl, my voice is too ethereal, lack grit, country or bland, and that my chords are too basic. When I was in specific churches, they tried to get me to "squall" and sing songs that were not a fit for me. So, you know what I did? I took my country white girl self to the "other" churches. *I stayed true to myself.*

What Church Do You Attend?

I have not been to church in four years. It was only during the process of writing this book that I went to a place of worship on March 17, 2019. I woke up one day, and before I could open my eyes, I saw a church building in my head. The day before, I was at the store, and a gentleman mentioned church, and I felt something. It was time to heal. These four years of being away from the visible church were necessary to clear out what I thought the church was and who I thought God was. It was hard and a process to separate Him from the leaders who represented him. In my mind, He allowed them to do ungodly things and seemingly get a pass and go on to flourish, while I suffered, for attempting to do the right

MY NEW LIFEWORK

thing. I needed to heal that mindset. This has been the dominant question asked of me since my return to social media, along with what church do I play at on Sundays. Mainly, people who knew me back then. That has always been intriguing to me as if that determines if you have a relationship with God based on your response. I'm sure people ask from a real place, or that's all they know to ask.

In this section, with compassion, I give you this notice that you may be triggered or triggered already, but hopefully not. It is my story, my experience. I hope that you read this darker side with patience until the end and throughout. Every detail shared is with purpose. Once you know it all, then you can better understand me, my stance and leave it at that. Here is a quick backdrop; raised in the church from a child, gave my life to God at the age of 15 and served as the music director/worship leader for 20 years. As a teen, my weekends consisted of rehearsals and church, no school activities, as I was, in church.

Also, in that 20-year space, I went at least four days out of the week or more depending on the event. I NEVER missed a service outside of Hurricane Allison, never took a vacation and only associated with other Christians. I was the First Lady of a church for seven years, read nothing but the Bible other than a few inspirational books, preached, taught, saw it all behind the scenes, met great people, lost some and became an ordained minister. I recorded a live praise and worship album where all the tracks recorded bled into each other once I took it to the studio for mixing and it was unfixable. That wasn't the engineer's fault, and I will leave it at that. I got my bachelor's degree in Counseling with a minor in Biblical Studies, can quote most of the Bible, and have always possessed an intense, passionate, and direct connection with God.

For years I was put in this box musically, spiritually and relationally. It was exhausting. Spiritual confinement kept my faith in a box. Being directed spiritually by a person who often had their translation or interpretation of what serving God meant, can stifle

FINISH IT

and bind a person from being free to serve God as they are led. We were told who to marry, and that we *must* marry, love or not, who to be friends with, what to name our kids. Very controlling in some places. I was taught to go out and reach the world, but subconsciously we were afraid to go out into the world because we thought we were going to become worldly or didn't feel spiritually equipped or grounded to do so. So, we just invited them to church. It becomes less daunting when we realize that the world that they are referring to are only people. People who are looking to be loved, cared for, and want to live their life. We were trained to invite them to church or ask what church they attended. For the longest, I was directed and felt trapped into thinking that every person I met, I had to mention Christ or invite them to church, or I had failed as a Christian. I walked around condemned for the rest of the day if I didn't meet my quota.

I am now starting to see that things that were uncomfortable or that did not feel right wasn't right, for me at least. Everything taught wasn't correct, and I have had to reconcile that. As soon as we get a whiff of a person that appears to be ungodly in our minds, we close ourselves off to so-call protect our faith or to not get tainted by worldly people or things of this life. Of course, no matter what your "religion" is or lack thereof, you must always protect yourself from anyone who would impact you negatively. We close ourselves off to the point where we say things like, "This is the Bible, it is what it is, and it is not up for debate." Some post things like, "This is not up for discussion, believe it or die and spend eternity in Hell." In this way, we block ourselves off from loving various types of people and meeting new people. I am shocked myself at my new circle of human beings. I talk, chat, hang and laugh with atheists, people of the LGBT+ community, Christians, non-Christians, Muslims, who and whatever! But it's hard to do that when you stay in the four walls of your church and denomination and seek to only bring them in instead of going out.

When you close yourself off like that and refuse to hear others or even have an intelligent dialogue, how do you expect them to be open to hearing anything you have to say? You get the same energy you put out, and you risk becoming self-righteous. I used to be like that. If I want someone to hear me out on anything, not just spiritual matters, I strive to hear them out. Therefore, I get the same in return. I have walked away from religion and tradition and what I have known to be the church. By the end of this book or in the future, that could change or not. I may find a fitting place. But this is my path right now, and I have peace with that and with the One that matters.

She Left Because She Was "Church Hurt"

She left because it was time to go. The last place of worship that I attended, where I spent years serving did not support the agenda for my life. I mean, dang. I was 35 years old and did nothing since I was 15, but play music, build, nurture, invest, and create for everybody else's ministry and church. And now there is an issue because I want to travel with my book and music and not step on their stage every week? When I tried to reach out via email, phone, text to see why people were acting funny or not speaking to me anymore, there was no response. Other than a non-verbal aura of- "If your agenda does not fit or line up with ours, on to the next one." So, I left. But right before I left, I was asked to write a whole youth curriculum after just spending ten months writing my first book. I said no because I wanted to do things outside of the walls, and one of the leaders walks off, upset??? I had everyone's full attention until I tried to do something different after 20 years. It's okay; rejection is always redirection. It had to be that way. I have nothing in my heart but love.

You know what? If you want to talk about church hurt, it hurt more to see other people treated poorly. People are tremendously

FINISH IT

helped, saved from destructive patterns, and shown a better way to live because of some churches — myself for one at one point in my life. I have a heart for people. These four years away has helped me clear false ideas about who God is and how he MUST be served.

People that feel or don't know how to think about me not going to church at this time in my life have no clue about me or my story and automatically assume it is church hurt. Initially, yes. It was hurtful to see how people were disposable. But at this point, I see there was a bigger purpose. People, you must be careful and very sensitive when trying to push others back to a place where they could have experienced the worst hurt in their life, and solely worrying about where they are on Sunday. And the threat of going to hell and having their blessings cut off is not appealing. For me, there were times it fell like hell *in* the church! Yes, there was hurt, and I am not exposing anybody in this book. Irrelevant and unnecessary. Know this! Because I am human too, I forgive any and every offense I experienced in those places.

Also, I am not anti-church. I am ANTI-RELIGION. And most of the people that invite me don't even want to go! And, they complain every week about the duties they have. Some people are fortunate enough to find solace at a place of worship, although not perfect, and I honor those people for where they are on their path. But this subject is too colossal for one book and one person to address, and that is not the point right now. But you would also be turned off if leaders you looked up to as spiritual leaders cut you off or fired you as their musician because you did not sleep with them or because I told another one not to text me after midnight unless it was church related. Umm...fired. Guess where I experienced domestic violence and sexual assault, and more than once? In the church. I felt shunned for wanting to expand my gifts outside of the walls. I could go on and on.

A higher purpose redirected me, and it has nothing to do with church hurt now. God is not in a box or only in those four walls. In

MY NEW LIFEWORK

other words, my gifts are not *just* for people of faith but people. I may be repeating myself, but not all churches and leaders are like that as some do have a heart for people. As I stated, I have visited a place of worship a few times recently, and it did bring about healing and closure for me during those visits. But no matter if I am/was in or out of the church, my Creator still loves and supports me unconditionally. Amazing!

I Was Always There, But Where Were You?

For over 20 years, I gave my life to help build other people's dreams and visions. But when I needed to heal or have someone there during my divorce or even to celebrate me when my first book took off, and I had to travel, I faced rejection because it did not fit their musical agenda. Some of the help I did receive had musical strings tied to them, or I was made to feel guilty for not serving in the house. Mind you; this was the directive, that service to the man of God or the house *is* service unto God. And back then my faith was somewhat toxic and unbalanced, so I did all I could to please the leader.

Now for the divorce part, in their defense, no one knew why I seemingly out of the blue filed for divorce. I did keep many things covered and private because as a Christian, especially a pastor's wife, you did not talk about the police coming to your house on more than one occasion. The shame of that. And the personality I have today was not that of yester-years. I was quiet. I did not know how to talk it out or who to talk to about it. So, when the church found out I filed for divorce, I was thoroughly rebuked as I expected and called into the office. I understand that because we wore those masks well and they had no clue of what was going on. But he and I joined this together, not God, and I speak more on this in my first book. Yes, I filed for divorce. I take full responsibility for choosing to get married to get out of my mom's house, to please

FINISH IT

the church as they were confident, we would fall into sexual sin and for lusting to be married. Yep, love had nothing to do with it at all. We both had ill-motives. But no one cared about why I was leaving, just that I was wrong for leaving. And I did not tell anyone before I filed because no one was going to talk me out of what I knew God told me and there are no regrets to this day!

I ONLY SAID YES BECAUSE HE ASKED

Whew. Breathe. Okay. I was going to jump to the day I filed for divorce. I knew something was missing but kept writing anyway. I cannot skip this because 21-year old Dorian needs to heal too. Here we go. Deep breath.

Meet Fox. No, that is not his real name, but he is real. When we met, neither one of us was in the healthiest place, certainly not in a position to get married. I was depressed, severely. Why? Because I was engaged to someone else, let's call him Pierre, two years before I met Fox. Pierre seemed perfect. I was only 18 when we connected. I was free, happy, singing around the city in a local group and then he approached me. We too were on our way to getting married, I thought. We complimented each other so well, and I started to attend Pierre's church. I was happy with him. He too was a minister. We studied the Bible together, and when he traveled to speak somewhere, I accompanied him for support or to play music before and after he preached. And he attended events where I would sing.

One night at Bible study during the benediction, we all grabbed hands for the ending prayer, and I felt it...in his hand. I knew. Something was off. We were together for about two years, and then he was gone. No explanation. No reason. He left the church that he brought me to and just ghosted me. That wasn't a popular term back then like it is today, but that is what he did. I called several

FINISH IT

times, and finally, he answered. He just gave a general response, like car or job issues, as to why he left and would not tell me anything else. That was not the truth.

What happened? No one had answers for me, not even him. I was in an unfamiliar place, lost, broken, and scared. I was not only depressed, but I was angry! You know why? Because I was so confused. We restrained from sex while engaged, trying to do the right thing according to the Christian faith, serving in the church together, and now God is saying no?! Boy, did I become bitter, sad, and my light was gone. It wasn't behind a man; it was because God was behind it. He could have stopped this.

I can feel the rage in me just like it was that year. After seeing the change in me after a while, the leaders of that institution pulled me into the office. Still, to this day, I don't know what the leaders told Pierre, but soon after that, he left the church. I assume they told him we were not supposed to be together. They noticed, their words exactly, "That I did not skip to the door anymore with joy." Can you imagine an 18-year-old skipping to the door of a church because they are so happy with life? That was me. I skipped. You would lose joy too if your heart were ripped from you and then told to get over it among some other things. I mean, I prayed and believed that the Divine was involved with us coming together — still left in the dark. Maybe there were red flags that I didn't see. But how in the world do you expect someone who for that length of time, that young and vulnerable to move on with no answers? But he proposed! Move on?! What the...?

Shattered and heartbroken, I kept going to the church without him. No joy. No life. No him. It was ten months later that a lady at the church asked me over to give her daughter piano lessons and, to talk. We were not close, so it was unusual. But I agreed. It was a Thursday. We talked, had lunch and she hit me with it. Whatever happened to you and Pierre? I was shocked but poured out my broken heart. Why is she doing this? Why does she care? I told

I ONLY SAID YES BECAUSE HE ASKED

her the leaders said to me that Pierre is not the one, and I needed to get him out of my system. She asked, "But what about what *you* know? What about what God told you two?"

I just broke. That is not even the kicker guys. Sunday comes. Guess who walks in?! Yep. Pierre! After ten months, he came to visit the church. I was in a better place, but it was still crazy! After service, out in the parking lot, the lady and I made eye contact. We were like, "WHAT?!" We looked at each other with our mouths opened. Talk about confusion. I did not speak to him, and it wasn't until months later when I was about to get married that we talked on the phone and met up.

But I Already Told Him Yes

Now here is where things get trickier. Later that Fall, I met Fox, through his friend. Fox asked me to marry him, and I said yes. I did not know him. I didn't love him, and he didn't love me. He asked me three weeks after we met.

I remember the day, so clearly the first time I saw him. I met his friend first at my job and discovered we were both musicians. It was a Friday night, and I was laying on my mom's couch with my hair all over the place. I was depressed, watching *Reba*. His friend called me and asked to meet up to play some music, and Fox was there. Honestly, he looked like he was going through some things himself.

The energy behind the proposal: He was a Christian. I was a Christian. "Will you submit to a husband?" he asked. I said, "Yes." He wanted a wife. I longed to get out of my moms' house. He served as a minister in the church. I served as a minister in the church. Let's get married. He believed I'd make a good First Lady. He studies the Bible. Yep. I hit the jackpot. I am still depressed from the last failed engagement, so maybe this is the answer. Let me pray. God, you are saying yes. So, okay. A union of convenience.

FINISH IT

Well, I said yes to his proposal, and it was four months of going back and forth, him deciding if I was the one, *after* he proposed. We were so young. What were we thinking? Here is your ring, then takes it back. He proposes again with the ring, then takes it back. It was non-stop for four months. He finally settled on his decision, but there was no love. No chemistry. No romance. Just religion. Almost like he was forced to marry me. Now don't get me wrong; we did not hate each other. But for some strange reason, we felt a duty or obligation to marry for ministry sake. Wrong! We too restrained from sex before marriage. We believed we were doing this for God, and sacrifices had to be made to save souls. Our gifts combined for the use of the Kingdom outweighed our true hearts desires. Wrong! At least it was wrong for us, for me. Our motives were self-centered and not rooted in love for God or each other. How could they be? We both loved other people.

During this process, Pierre and I talked on the phone, and I gave him the "exciting" news. He asked, "What about us? What God said about us?" Followed by several, "Are you sure's?" I'm like, *what*? By that time, I was over it. Not healed, but over it and now you want to talk to me? Now you want to ask me that. My reply, "But I already told him yes." I remember Pierre asking me if I loved my new future husband. "Do you love him?" I repeated, "I already told him yes." I'm a woman of my word. CRAZY! I was numb, lost, and more excited about the move than I was about marrying my new partner. I packed my truck with all my belongings and went to meet Pierre one last time. I wasn't the same Dorian. The way things went down changed me. He could not reach me no matter what he said. But we sat in his car, talked, kissed, and said our goodbyes. The kiss said it all. I was making a mistake, and my heart was still there. But the Dorian he knew was not. If only I had of healed correctly. This Dorian was still bitter and angry with him. So, in her ego, she marries someone she didn't know or love.

I was happy because somebody asked me to marry them, so I rolled with it. But I felt out of control. I knew my heart was still with Pierre, but my ego, wounds, and fear of him doing it again pulled me in another direction. What if no one else ever proposes? And you, Pierre, didn't want to marry me, so. And you aren't even fighting for me now! Are you just going to let me go? You just let me go. I wanted to hear that you loved me and don't marry him! Statements, not questions. We said our goodbyes and that was that.

Also, my family assumed I knew what I was doing because I was a church-girl who read her Bible and prayed. I later found out that everyone around me shook their heads inwardly and could not see me marrying Fox. I wasn't going to listen anyway. I just wanted to be married. Matter of fact, whenever he would go back and forth, I would pray thinking that Satan was trying to steal what God had for me. I left Pierre's church and the new church I was attending persuaded me that it was indeed Satan trying to take my blessing. I know. Toxic. Toxic faith. I wanted to be married so bad that I could not see that the back and forth was protection, redirection and NO! To me, it was yes, period. I was running and running from me.

Even though Pierre and I did not end up together, I realized that he was perfect for *that* Dorian, and I was *more* in love with love and marriage than I was with him.

I tried to speak. You wouldn't listen. So, I write.

Let me say this if anybody has an issue with anything I say in *my* book about any part of my journey; that is not on me. I reached out, emailed, texted, asked to meet with you, called and begged for answers, left voicemails in tears asking for clarity and closure. My statement is not just in relationships but with other parts of my story as well that I will speak on later. No response. No one would listen. So, I write.

FINISH IT

Let's continue. Fox's family told me not to marry him. They knew he still loved his ex. I've never been the type that goes after the other girl, especially if he is pursuing her. But being in the same place often, she and I had a few talks about the ordeal. This before he and I married as he kept going back to her. She was not the issue. Following his heart was. I had nothing ill to say about her. She was a beautiful young lady who wanted to follow her heart as well. She loved and cared about him. I barely knew him.

They probably would've been happy together. But we looked better together according to the church, a better fit as far as what a pastor and first lady should look like. I believed we convinced ourselves it was the right thing to do. It wasn't. It was 30 days, just a month into that marriage that I again realized I had made a mistake. But I stayed for seven years and so did she, meaning, he held on to her. I could feel it. If only we both were walking in our true authentic self. He should have followed love, and I should have waited for it.

THE DAY I FILED

I will share my process of separation, divorce, and rebuilding. As far as the seven years that I was married, I will bypass the happenings of that season. I was not with the right person, which explains everything. We were not right for each other. That heals me and gives me closure. He is a human being who also had his life turned upside down, experienced pain, and only wanted to be loved like we all deserve to be loved. I'm sure he thought he was doing the right thing based on social conditioning and what religion tells us we are to do. Plus, I have two beautiful gifts that came of it. That is all that matters. Often, it is not that he or she is an evil person. We think that based on the tumultuous and negative things that take place year after year in the relationship. Why are we so afraid to admit that we made a mistake or a choice based on something other than love? And that we're not with the person we are supposed to be with or that our heart desires? Probably because to fix it may be just as messy. And going after true love, joy, and fulfillment, whether to be alone as a single person or with someone else, is scary.

We are not sure if it is worth the cost. After all, we had a home together, two kids, time spent, fighting to keep it together, fighting to fight…fighting out of misery and no one could explain the consistent discord other than the devil is trying to steal your marriage. What will people think? We are leaders. We are Christians. I need to pray through it and watch God move. But He doesn't in a lot of cases. And that is a hard truth for many of us to swallow so we stay and leave our kids in toxic situations because we don't want them in separate homes, the back and forth visitations, other people doing our kids hair…etc. We stay and watch our kids run to the phone to call 911 because mom and dad are going at it again, the yelling, the anger, the violence, the trauma…all because God hates divorce?

Others will choose to stay and love the one they are with. That is their choice, especially if things are "okay," or workable, it's not *that* bad, there's peace, so why rock the boat, right? There is no passion, but there is peace. That is their mindset. They will settle for external peace while inwardly there is frustration and conflict. I've seen those cases (mine to be honest), and people stay together for years, possibly loving someone else secretly, choosing to do what they feel is the honorable thing by keeping the family together, until some tire of that life and step out while still maintaining a household.

We have side people and relationships, even in the church, because the love is gone or was never there and it is now a celibate marriage. So, let's cheat on the other person (emotionally/physically) but stay together for years instead of doing what must be done to live a life of truth, honesty, and integrity. Yes, let's stay together because of the kids, finances, obligation because we made

FINISH IT

a past vow but are living a lie now. We dare not face the truth with our partners but choose to live in misery, looking outside of the marriage, enduring internal conflict daily. We're trapped. We get marital help; it gets better for a few days or weeks, and then it is back to the same cycle over and over. That is a huge red flag. And check this out. It can be both partners feeling this way, not just one. I have lived it. Freedom starts with the truth, and that doesn't mean it still can't work out. But you must face and speak the truth to yourself. That's if you want to be free. My truth led me on the path I took and where I am today. For me, I would've suffered loss, whether I stayed or left. It was difficult either way. I could've stayed and lost out on true love, tranquility, and divine destiny. Or left as I did, and lost material things that I have replaced with better and it's about to get even better! But which path gave me inner peace, authenticity, and the one where I did not have to wear a mask? Which was the best route for my children?

I know I chose the right path because as of today, nothing has changed as far as how we interact. He is who he is, and I am who I am. And I remember when talking to God during my decision process to leave or stay, Him showing me almost silently that, "Dorian, nothing has changed. He is not going to change who he is. This is who you chose." I remember asking if he or it would *ever* change? The answer was no. At least not for me he would, because he wasn't meant to change. Now I see how people can come back together and *really* make it work, *really* be in love and rebuild even after a separation or divorce. When it's meant to be, people go their separate ways, change, admit their wrongs, see their mistakes, heal and come back together as different/better versions of themselves. Both people must be willing to see what needs to change and not because there is a threat of loss which I experienced. In my case, during any separation and reconciliation, change was temporary. There'd be reconciliation but not a pure one. There was a need or loss at stake rooted in self-interest. But if I had stayed, I would still be dealing with the same dynamic with him as I am dealing with to this day.

Remember, this is not for everyone, but it is for someone. I get it. Reconciliation and working it out is always the first and best choice. That's what we always hear. But that is unfair and unjust to those who are sincerely struggling and have a different path. We don't want to face the reality that these situations are a result of a decision we made to get married in the first place that was not pure or divinely guided. We can debate that just because it starts wrong, doesn't mean that God can't make it right. Well, anything is possible. But *so* many people are left in marriages/relationships because we don't address the ones that are not supposed to continue. Maybe start at the beginning. Look at the motives, reasons, circumstances that brought you together. Just start there. You may find that healing the beginning brings about reconciliation and an even stronger union or bring you to the realization that this needs to end.

I Should Not Have

Where do we get off thinking that it is our purpose to stay in misery when one or both parties refuse to do the work, year after year? Or when you know deep down, it's not right? We stay because someone else tells us it's better for us. And they're probably miserable themselves in their relationship or do not understand your situation or path. So, I should have stayed and taught my kids that it's okay to stay with someone who does not love you because of society and religion? Teach my daughter that someone else's comfort is worth more than yours? Teach them that pleasing people trumps divine fulfillment? Make no mistake. I stayed seven years, and that is with counseling from every top preacher in our city, conferences, books, cd's and cassette tapes at that time on marriage, prayer, you name it. So, <u>I am not promoting divorce</u>. I do find it odd that we can admit that we should not have paid that much for that car, should not have gone to college for that course of study, should not have quit that job or moved, or went into business with that person.

But we can't admit that we should not have married that person and that we should have waited? Doesn't mean it has to end but it's about getting to the root of the issue so the marriage can have a real chance. I fought to keep mine alive, but a plant can't survive, planted in the wrong soil and the wrong pot, no matter what you do. It is and was only natural for me to "fight for my marriage," as you hear people say, even though that was not *my* divine marriage. People to this day are fighting for things that they should release, but it's a process to see that. It's natural to consider it yours because of the vows, investments, our faith, our fear, fear of loss, etc. I mean, we want to win, not lose. So, if you know someone who is fighting for theirs, graciously let them even if history and patterns prove it's just another dead-end cycle. We all must learn our lessons. One day, they will like me, get hit with the question, "You had enough yet?"

I was perplexed when I finally decided to leave, and the pastor rebuked me while in counseling, saying that I was out of the will of God for leaving. This same pastor was currently married to his "first love" from back in the day. But they separated when they were younger. He married someone else, it was hell, and they divorced. Then the "first love" came back into the picture, and they are now together flourishing with happily ever after's...And I even brought that up in the session. But what did I get? The Bible text, what God has joined together, let no man separate... Great. Well, God did not join us together; I did. We did. I can't say this enough. All we needed was the shotgun (shotgun wedding). I was so desperate that I paid for the rings, the license, and the honeymoon after our courthouse wedding. It takes two, both parties to want it. As short as this life is, I refuse to spend year after year begging and pleading to be loved and fulfilled. It is too many people out here for that.

And I'm going to waste my life, behind a contract, a paper that the other party has already disregarded in words, actions and deeds? No one honors the bond of marriage more than me, seeing that I've been trying to be married since I was five. I love it! But I will not be miserable, and I've done too much work on myself to be unhappy, ever again. **I cringe at the thought of being coerced, in the name of God, to stay in that marriage. In other words, you mean to tell me, that God was saying, "Dorian, I know he is emotionally connected to someone and would rather be with her, and there's constant discord, but I hate divorce. I want you to stay in a loveless, sexless marriage because I hate divorce. So just settle and make it work."** I tried that, and it didn't work. I don't want to have to *make* anything work. I want something that just works! And if there is a vision of what that looks like in my heart and mind, that means it exists, and it exists for me. So, I'm waiting for it.

I know this is touchy, but I am not afraid to touch it because it may not resonate with all, but it will with some. If not, as for me, I realized that I made a mistake. And for a while, I stayed thinking I deserved that circumstance as punishment. That's what I get. No Dorian, you can course correct, and everything has worked out just fine. We all have our journey.

Why do we stay in situations where we see it's not right for us? Of course, there are many answers to that question, and timing comes into play. But I don't have to stay anywhere if my heart is telling me otherwise and I don't care what religion, society, a clergyman or anyone says. Our heart, feelings, and intuition are there for a reason. We save ourselves so much heartache when we live from the heart. I respect the view of another, but I am accountable for my own life. I hope you have not closed the book by now because you disagree, but it could be because I did not reveal all

FINISH IT

that happened during those seven years. If you knew, I promise you, you would agree. Both parties have moved on. I respect the dynamic we have now not to air that information.

If you want to unwisely take this as an out for you just because you are "not happy", that is on you. I will not be there for whatever the consequences are just as no one was there with me, which is what I wanted. I wanted this to be my decision. I was ready to face whatever as a result. I just wanted out! You must know in your *knowing* what is right for you.

High-fives and kudos to those who have overcome this and stuck it out or those who divorced and remarried each other all over again. Yes! That is your path. I celebrate you if you are in your bliss. Let's not condemn or judge another who does not have that path. Let's say, yes to them as well because it takes a lot to overcome in these cases and to rebuild such as myself. It takes just as much or even more grit. I celebrate my bliss if no one else does. I say yes to myself. Good girl Dorian! You rebuilt your life by yourself for the last ten years. You have two tenacious children that are golden, not perfect, but they make it easy for me. They are now in high school. To this day, I have yet to get a call from the school since elementary about grades or behavior for either one of them. Good job, Dorian.

But I get it. It's not easy to reconcile all of this when children are involved and assets as well. I have been there. I had to let go of social conditioning, religion, tradition, and my own unhealthy thoughts of what was right or what people would think of my choice. All of that was no longer serving me but keeping me trapped. It was time to go.

IT'S TIME TO GO

The last year of that marriage, I told myself that I would take that year to see if anything would change. I sat back and watched. I took notes, literally. I took note of the rituals, the motions of raising kids while lacking a marital connection, and that for years. I noted how many times *her* name came up…again. And how I was made to look crazy questioning how one always knew *her* current status in life, every year of our marriage. But I get it now. It crushed me then, but his heart was with her. I was not where he wanted to be. I wasn't defeated because I was so in love with him. I felt defeated because this marriage that I ran to did not remedy my fantasy. That's what crushed me. Back then I believed like so many that marriage was the remedy to all the things I did not get in my other relationships. Nope. There was a deeper issue.

He and I both stayed for the sake of not quitting, for stability, the children, and the church. But it was a toxic, karmic and co-dependent relationship. That last year, I put my all into it as I did every year. Around November, I made my decision. It was time to go. Honestly, there were seven different times in those seven years that it was "time to go". But I stayed too long. I listened to the wrong voice(s). I had plenty of outs, but I had to learn my lesson. I prayed back in what God had already sent out. I opened the door that He was trying to shut. I followed religion and legalism instead of following my heart. When he walked out, more than once, seven to be exact, I still didn't get it. I looked over my notes for that year, and things I asked for to help us as a couple, went unaddressed. And we are arguing about *her*…again???

Here is what was fascinating to me. I knew things were changing that last year when I was looking into the future, seeing myself performing music on stage. I did not see Fox anywhere. It was like his person, or his energy was not in my outlook. I just saw myself without him. I felt like I was waking up from a seven-year nap.

After six years of the same and some severe situations, the last few years just started to feel like extreme blah. You could see parenting, ministering, and working, but no romance, affection, or passion. In all honesty, it began with blah. I cannot say the romance left because it was never there.

FINISH IT

I'm Leaving: The Final Days

After a conversation with someone, I realized that I needed closure on why I married him, who and what was I running from and where and who was my real divine partner. Or maybe I was meant to be single. I don't even remember what we were talking about, but it was random, and she asked me one question. The same question the lady asked me from that church! "Did you ever have closure with Pierre? And why do you think *she* keeps coming up in your marriage?" My heart sank. I dropped the phone and dropped to my knees. Everything dropped. It was as if the answer hit me right in the abdomen. Immediately, I knew that I was going to leave him. I did not know how, who, or what. I just knew. For the first time in that marriage, I felt empowered to do what was right for me, as if the veil was lifted. I told him my plans around Thanksgiving, and I filed for divorce around Christmas. Mind you, I was a mother of a four and five-year-old, no college degrees, was running a licensed home daycare with only a few kids, and it was not enough to support myself, along with being a church musician. Leaving was a leap of faith for me.

Time out: Let's address Pierre, in case you are wondering. Here is what I understand. Sometimes things are meant to be, but we have free will to choose. If we don't, the Universe will put us on a course correction or replace someone if need be who *will* choose. Other times divine destiny overrides our free will. Sometimes people are just lessons. The reason Pierre came up as questions from these ladies before I got married and right at the end of that marriage, was to remind me of the joy I felt loving someone and waiting for it this time. I am confident he is not the one, but a reminder to use that experience as a gauge next time and to not settle. Make sure it's mutual. Even with Fox, there was the feeling of duty, not love surrounding our connection. That is not my love story. Pierre is my lesson on WAITING, as well as that marriage.

A Year of Blah

The timing of my departure is probably going to shock most of you. But when asked what happened during that year that I decided to leave, my answer is not the usual response. Was it the physical altercations? The misuse of money, or did it have to do with *her* again? The answer is no to all those questions. That did not take place *that* year. Nothing was going on. It was a year of blah, peace, no cops, mundane, no action, physically, intimately, or emotionally. You would think I would have left at a time when all the answers to those questions were yes during the marriage. But no. It was early Fall; I overheard him on the phone, well right in front of me, ask someone about how *she* was doing. He tried to play it off as if it was no big deal, and that set me off after all I had forgiven. Which then led me to have that conversation with the person who made me drop to my knees.

Agree or disagree, it is not always those top three, cheating, beating, or stealing that gives you an out in a marriage. Therefore, people who want to leave struggle with indecisiveness because we are taught that to leave due to "irreconcilable differences" is weak and not of God. In other words, there must be extreme reasons to divorce according to the church and society. I am aware of the scriptures for those who are ready to hit me with the Bible. I am aware of people who will stay and pray through it all, drag-outs, kicked out, outside pregnancies, etc. I am aware. Forgiveness is beautiful.

Anyhow, what if, plainly put, this is not your "person"? I think the lack of passion, inspiration, disconnect, and negativity (internal) is just as much a red flag as the chaos, drama, and constant fighting (external). In my case, we had all the flags, including physical altercations. I believe both are signs that this may not be the person, and both are unhealthy environments for the parties involved, including the children. I'd rather have my children raised as they were with one parent in the home over what they saw as young children. He

FINISH IT

was gone so much; it was like I was a single mother anyway. Man, just writing that statement gives me insight. He did not want to be there. He wanted to be free. That is sad. To feel trapped. I will confess this. There were times when he would leave for hours and even months, and I had not heard from him. My heart was hoping he would not return and that he was with Jesus. I am dead serious. I even prayed that God would take him so I could be free too. I only thought that way because I was too scared to leave on my own. I wanted God to fix it. But He was not going to fix what I created.

I look back and see a mediocre and uninspired life during much of that marital season. It was so hard, barren, and at times, full of nothingness. I was living someone else's life. Again, people ask if I had any feelings for Fox when I made my decision. No, I did not. I did not love him, and I honestly did not even like him as a person. How could I after such harsh treatment throughout those years? I was indifferent, which is worse than hate or anger to me. I felt neither at the time. That is how I knew it was over. That is why I say my story may not be yours. Years after the divorce, I thought about all the times I was left and abandoned, before, during, and after the kids. Those were dark times, and I stayed faithful until he came back. So, no. I do not feel bad for leaving. Man, karma really is a…You reap what you sow and some.

Couples get to this point in their marriage but still have feelings and care about each other. Or at least one party does. Great! There could be a chance. But what baffles me, is that every time, we separated, and it was plenty of times, we always came back for reasons other than love. I'm still processing that. Let's see, we came back because of the church, then because of the kids and the sake of family, or it would serve us better financially, or he had no place to live. Not one time was it because we could not live without each other and loved one another so much.

You know, co-dependency is real even in marriages like the one I had. Individuals will stay because it benefits them and not necessarily you or because of love. They must have someone or can't be without a relationship. *Mom already has people living with her, so I can't go there. So, let me live with my spouse who I don't care for that much, but it helps me out financially,* some will rationalize. It is a tough pill to swallow, knowing someone is with you for reasons other than candid love.

"Cheaper to keep her," they say, but it may cost you even more down the line if you seek "solace" in another because you weren't satisfied. You can end up getting caught, with an unexpected pregnancy, with an STI, dead, etc. When all you had to do was be honest about what's in your heart no matter what you think you will lose. You stand a better chance at a peaceful resolution in going your separate ways versus your partner finding out you weren't happy and used them while you sought love elsewhere. Start with honesty. You know what else? It doesn't mean there's always someone else in the picture. Sometimes it's harder to face your partner with the truth that you just don't want to be with *them*. Keep reading.

Just Me and God

So, for Thanksgiving that final year, I cooked the grandest meal I had ever made. I cooked all his favorite dishes and some. Now, back then, I was intimidated and stayed away from the entrees that mom, aunties, and grandma would make. And I was not much of a soul food eater. I was not much of a cook, to be honest. But I was inspired by the idea of a new life. I went back and looked at a home video that I still have while writing this section and here is what I prepared: rolls, fruit salad, cornbread dressing, greens, a broccoli and cheese casserole with spicy sausage, green beans and potatoes, yams, corn, cranberry sauce, macaroni and cheese, corn and a huge ham! There was so much food, and most I had cooked for the first time! I had to give some of it away. The reviews were

FINISH IT

great, and I have bragging rights to this day. Then I told him I was divorcing him.

Late December, I went away for a weekend to reflect on my decision and how my life was about to change and made a deal with God. By then the negotiations had begun, thirty days of negotiations: *"I will do this better"*, get a gym membership, a surprise hotel stay for two and so much more. It was too late. I was already gone mentally, spiritually, and emotionally. That weekend was powerful. As a mother of two young kids and all the other hats I wore in seven years, I had never had time to myself like that. Ever. It was an issue at first for me to go away, but it was either let me go and get clarity or I will leave now. By then, I had found my voice. My sister dropped me off to get a rental car, and I was off to fast, pray, meditate, and go within. These were my exact words: *God; I am going to get a divorce. I know what people are saying and what the leaders have taught, but I am leaving. You don't ever have to use me again to sing, play, or speak in front of anyone if I get to take care of my kids and be at peace with You.*

I already knew in my heart what I was going to do, so I did not go away to ask. I went away to hear in peace what my heart was guiding me to do and to give God one more chance to show me if I was crazy. Nope, total peace. I came back home and started planning my exit. First, I had a daycare in my home with six kids, four in the daytime and two after school. This information is significant later in the story. How in the world was I going to be able to file if I work from home through the week? Second, where was I going to get and spend $250.00 without push back? I stepped down as the musician at our church, as I was going through so many internal changes and conflict. There was a battle of truth/heart vs. logic/religion. I didn't want to be in the forefront at that time. It just didn't resonate with me to play, making my only income the daycare. I prayed that if this was supposed to happen, He was going to have to guide and provide and that will be my confirmation. It was December 23rd the day I filed, but that Thursday before, our church called and asked if I would play for their afternoon service. Guess how much they paid me? Yep, $250.00! I immediately knew this was my sign...and then I started to shake.

Now, how will I get downtown to file with these kids? Believe it or not, it was a rainy day (so cliché), and every one of my parents called and said they would be running late the day I wanted to go. Wow. I was in shock but needed to move fast. I was fighting myself the whole way. What about the traffic on I-10? Plus, I had my own two kids with me. Well, when I got on the freeway at 8 a.m., there was no traffic. Anyone who knows about I-10 in the Katy/Houston area knows what an abomination it can be. I shook more and more. But what about parking? Parking was a big one. I had never really driven downtown or parked because I was scared and sheltered until the age of 28, the year I filed. And I just really started to break out of my shell at age 37.

Of course, I found a spot with ease, and I did not drive the wrong direction as I had before once upon a time, into oncoming traffic. Well, what about the rain, getting the kids out, and walking across the street? My kids were playing in the droplets which they never did. Surely there was going to be a long line. Nope. I was the only one filing for divorce the day before Christmas Eve in my county. I kid you not! When I saw that empty lobby, I was speechless. I walked to the window with the paperwork that I filled out. I could not speak. I handed her the paper visibly shaking. The lady at the window asked if I was okay. Life was about to change, and I didn't know how. I remember her slamming that "filed" stamp on my paperwork. I jumped, and that was it.

We get into the car and head back, hoping I would not have parents waiting for me. I was five minutes from the house, the rain stopped, and each parent called one by one to say they were on their way. True story. I was thrilled! I did it! Of course, all hell broke loose for the next year and a half, which is how long it took

FINISH IT

to finalize everything. Again, information about what happened during the divorce process will remain private. But I will tell you I experienced panic attacks for the first time. I thought the seven years were tumultuous. Man, that was child's play compared to the confirmations I received that I was indeed doing the right thing, meaning I saw a hidden side of a lot of people. I also know, in times of desperation and the fear of losing it all can make a person do crazy things. It was a fight for my life. And not just humanly speaking. There were negative and dark entities that did not want to let me go and operated through people to try to keep me in that situation. And you know what? I didn't have the backing of the church or church family at that time. The Universe sent new people, angels, unexpected individuals whom you will hear about in a bit.

I think I was more afraid of the court process. This country girl wasn't used to the system. Other than the cops frequenting our home, I had never encountered the legal system and for that long. I was petrified every time in the beginning, visibly shaking at times and would barely talk or look anyone in the eye. I had never experienced anything like this. But by the end of it all, I had found my voice and was ready to square up. My lawyer had to tell me to be quiet a few times. I was sick of it. That is where I learned how to *Talk it Out*! I'm so proud of myself.

And here I am today. Yeah, I know, to file right before Christmas Eve. It was now or never. You all see me as I am now, but back then, I was timid, quiet, reserved, and an introvert unless I was singing. So, to stand up for me in this situation was terrifying! How was a single mother with no other life experience other than playing for a church going to make it on her own? And no one knew what I was doing initially. No one. It was just God and me.

Now. Let's get this straight. I left that marriage because I did not want to be with him anymore. Period. I was single most of that marriage anyway. If there were someone else, I probably would have still been with them. Not only that, I know me. I've never cheated in any relationship! I will leave you first before I cheat, which is what I did. I left. I didn't have enough self-worth to cheat, nor did men ever approach me. Meaning, I didn't feel good about myself, so I didn't attract anyone and was too miserable to even think about that. I just wanted out. Either way, I was going to leave whether I got closure from someone else or not. My mind was made up from that call in November. I woke up. And it did not matter if I was leaving to be with six people; I was not staying there! I left for the sake of moving on with my life! Boy, sometimes the Sunnyside H-town in me just wants to…breathe…but I am going to continue as the refined Dorian and finish this book.

Where were we? Oh yes, let me change that. I did leave Fox for someone else. I left him for me, to reunite with Dorian. (Fyi, I was born as, Dorin.) I added an 'a' after my divorce because people had been pronouncing it wrong since I was a kid. People thought and still do think that I am a man until they see or hear me. I regularly deal with "May I speak to Mr. Dorin Watson" over the phone and on my mail. But *Dorian*? That name changed my whole identity.

You know what else? My life didn't start to move until I became Dorian Watson again. I remember the day the papers were final and I saw my name in print, getting this sense or as if Heaven was saying, "Now you can pick up where you left off because what I have planned was and has always been for Dorian Watson, not Dorin "X". We've been waiting for her." Yes, there was a purpose, lessons learned, my children, and growth in so many areas. Before I married, I was a manager of a bookstore, owned a vehicle, had money in the bank, pretty good credit, etc. But projects that I attempted during that marriage, never came to fruition. No advancements in any careers or education, poor to fair credit, broke, lack of travel, drama and constant evictions. There was no blessing, no highlights, other than my children. And if you recall at the beginning of the book, all my significant and major steppingstones happened after my divorce and after my course correction. No wonder nothing in my life ever prospered during that connection. It was time to go.

One scene I forgot to mention was when I drove and sat in the grocery store parking lot in our neighborhood. It was after I went away for final clarity. It was nighttime, quiet. I was in shock that all this time, I was in the wrong place. I wept it seemed like seven years' worth of tears. It is ironic, but they were tears of peace, explanation, and understanding. As I cried, so many flashbacks of the marriage popped in my head. That's why that happened, and that's why this happened. So much lost time and distance from family and friends because of this marriage. Even God and I used to be closer, but my connection with Him felt distant all those years. He was there, but it was not the same. We didn't speak much in the car. I believe my healing began instead. Although my eyes filled with tears, I could see clearly at that moment. It finally all made sense. I *was* loveable. I *was* worthy. I *wasn't* forgotten or exiled. I was just in the wrong place. I looked up and felt like Heaven silently asked me if I had had enough yet? I nodded my head, though I heard no voice, wiped my face, headed back, and filed the next day.

The Aftermath

My ex already had plans that I didn't know about, to stay somewhere else, seeing that I was leaving. Remember, I filed in December. Convincing me to renew our lease together in January, I was left stuck in that lease, that I could not afford alone. I remember sitting with that pen in my hand feeling uneasy about signing that paper. If we'd only follow our spirit and intuition! The idea was to let the kids still stay in the home, and both incomes were required for that to happen. But I didn't care about that. I was willing to stay with my sister if necessary.

Well, the kids and I had to move anyway. Nevertheless, someone helped me get an apartment by paying the deposit, and she allowed

I ONLY SAID YES BECAUSE HE ASKED

me to pay her back when I could. And I did. Thank you, T.P. I got a job working for a church, but that didn't work out. I will leave that alone. So consequently, I was evicted from my apartment after only four months. It hurt that a faith leader was behind my termination. I could not go home because my mom had people living with her. We had nowhere to go. Seriously. So, LaShawn G., who was on the first album I attempted to release, took us in to stay in her son's room when I had nowhere to go. LaShawn was a single mother of two herself but offered her home to us. I was so lost. She had been divorced and was sent to help me navigate this terrifying new path. So grateful for her, the long talks, her readiness to fight someone, anyone, on my behalf, and just being there with no judgment. Here is what I am saying. People may not understand why others get divorced or say that God will not bless them, or you guys need to work it out. But sometimes, it just does not work out. And God will send angels along the way to give you a down payment, a place to stay, and even a job. A few months after moving in with her and losing that job, I ended up working for another church.

This pastor, Pastor A.B., another angel, found an affordable house for me to rent. I was in the middle of my divorce and needed a place to live. If I have not said this yet, I never said that it was a walk in the park when I made my decision or that it would be. There were losses, but the gain far outweighs that. This pastor always looked out for us, asking if the kids and I needed anything during my two years there. There was another leader I remember who took me in and was willing to hide me in his church to protect me. I see now that it is not unusual for people to stalk or follow someone else during traumatic times of loss or change. We all cope differently. But sometimes people are just nuts. Someone even sent pictures of me taken without my knowledge that I still have. Man, I was skinny. I digress. Yeah, it was hard for him to let go of all this, (just kidding, trying to lighten the mood here guys).

FINISH IT

Then there is my first, Pastor F.D. This was the first church I ever played in as a teenager. He put a chair in the front row even though it did not match the pews where his family sat (and we were on TV, but that didn't matter to him). I told him it was hard to hear him preach because I was sitting behind him when I came down from the organ. This man taught me the foundation of faith, and I honor him for that. Always. I still regard my spiritual foundation, regardless of where I am today. I am not one to say that all pastor's or churches are evil. I am just telling my story.

In the aftermath, I lost friends, church associates, my mind, at times, endured panic attacks and lost my good credit. But I never imagined I would be where I am today. And this does not compare to where I know I will go from here. And by the way, I was able to build my desired home after restoring my credit on my own to almost 800. I even started a credit restoration business. It is going to be okay. I promise. Now, there is a way to do things so that you can have a positive result.

Meaning, I considered it, made my choice, and sat my partner down. I made my choice first because it was not about another lover. I'm confident that even in the aftermath, all is well today because I did it right. You may say that it was so hard for me because I was wrong for leaving and it should have been a breeze. That's not true in any area of life. Whenever we try to start a business, go back to school, whatever we take on to make our lives better, there will be challenges. That's what makes it a compelling "trials to triumph" story. No one wants to hear how good you had it all your life and that's what got you here because that's not the story of most of the world. And one thing I now reflect on is that I NEVER not ONCE second guessed myself no matter how hard it was for us. Between the job loss, eviction, government assistance, and the financial hits, I never wanted to go back, nor did I look back. There were no conversations about us trying again on my end. I was done. Whatever I went through to leave that situation, was better than staying. **Yes, it was challenging at the start, but every step of the way, every need was met!** Let's not talk about how I could afford a lawyer with a job loss, and how there was a zero balance/paid in full receipt by the time the ink dried on my divorce decree! He was not cheap and was very successful. Baby girl was in the right place now!

Anyway, I was upfront and told him out front; I am leaving. I didn't play with his feelings or go back and forth. It didn't matter what emotional response he gave me, anger, frustration, wrath, empty threats, attempted nostalgic triggers, or pleas of negotiation. My stance remained; I am leaving. I made sure I was at the point that there was nothing he could say or do. That is how I knew it was over. I knew when he was full of various emotions, and I had none that this cycle in my life had closed. When a Scorpio is done, they are done.

I just looked at him no matter the reaction projected at me until he let it all out. Where was all this fight and passion during these seven years? Lastly, no one else was involved, not even my friends. True story. All my connections and my friends at the time started blowing up my phone because no one knew what I did until he told them. "YOU DID WHAT?!?!" was pretty much the message on the back to back phone calls I received. They were shocked that I did it but also wondered what took so long. Despite the situation, I was a faithful, loyal, present wife. That is just who I am, and only a few know what went on behind closed doors. I have no remorse or regret. I deserved better.

A NEW PERSPECTIVE FOR ME

My Faith

I have learned that my mission is not to save the world. That is not my job. My job is to love people, and people of every race, culture, and faith, no matter where they are in life. I was so closed off from non-Christians and afraid that I was going to be tainted when I was religious. But if we are spiritually grounded, what is the harm in hearing another's story? If a person is of another faith, atheist or believes in tarot cards or crystals, most Christians will not even say hello to them. I used to be like that thinking I was like Jesus. But he didn't act like that!

Zacchaeus in the Bible was known as a wicked person, and Jesus voluntarily went to his house, did not say anything about what Zacchaeus was doing or how he lived. Zacchaeus changed his lifestyle just by Jesus being there. Do you think people are unaware that they are making unhealthy decisions and hurting themselves? Do you suppose always telling them about their life is going to fix it? That repels them. This time around, I am just going to *be there*. Just be there and let whatever happens, happen. In other words, I have stepped down from my religious legalistic high horse and can now be of some earthly good.

A NEW PERSPECTIVE FOR ME

Funny how Jesus did not announce himself to Zacchaeus. He tried to avoid attention. It was just something about him. He was just there.

I am adjusting to allowing myself to experience life, my liberties, and freedom as a human being without fear of damnation. For over 20 years, that is all I ever heard, "Don't, don't and don't or you are going to hell." If I attended your church, this is not a shot at you. I am speaking of the culture of the church on a broader scale. Remember, as you read *my* story and *my* experiences, they are not everyone's experience or journey. It is my path for my life, my book, and my freedom of speech — no need to disdain the church or people of any faith. I went through what I went through for a reason. I have nothing in my heart but love for everyone.

I want to live. And if there is a lesson I need to learn, let me learn it. People that live freely are much happier than those who feel they must repent for every move they make that seems wrong. Or continuously have in the back of their mind they are sinning all the time. No exaggeration. I lived like that, and I attended a church with that doctrine. You are much happier when you live your life instead of sitting in judgment of yourself and others. One leader told me that while I am playing the keyboard if I hit a wrong note, there must be sin in my life. Young, afraid, vulnerable, with an overwhelming ache to please God, I believed many things I should not have. Unhealed places in me caused me to use the church as a crutch, and I was co-dependent on religion.

My friend D.D. says it like this, "*Recovery from those rigid ways of seeing God, takes time. You have the voice of the past that critiques who you are becoming. We are so entrenched in that world view as we have spent most of our lives in that space. As you continue to move forward knowing that who you are becoming is sacred, and powerful, it is still God speaking and moving you forward on your faith journey. It takes time for you to move forward*

FINISH IT

with confidence that all that is happening as "strange" as it may feel is God."

I am not a part of a church as far as the institution or building. Who knows if I ever will be again? As I said, I did visit a place a few weeks ago after four years. And if after reading this you think, "Man, she needs to come to my church, we don't have all that foolishness, and she would love it", you are missing the point. I remember sitting and talking to Julius for three hours about my journey and life in the church. And you know what I appreciated about him the most? Is that he didn't invite me to his. He softly said, "I understand where you are." No smug look or "Humph". Just space for me to be where I am.

Am I against someone inviting me to their church? No. I am talking about when someone tells you their story, and they share their pain, or their experience and a person automatically thinks that person needs to be in a church for healing. That may be the answer for some. There are genuine and sincere people that request for you to visit their place of worship. I used to be one of them. What is dangerous and unfortunate is when people try to get me to go back to a place that I have healed from based on their legalistic and religious mindset, without taking the time to ask about my journey and where I am now.

SILENT TREATMENT

When I left the church, I had to process a lot of things. I questioned things or had what people call a crisis of faith. For the most part, when you work for a company for 20 years, you walk away with something to show for your dedication and to prove you were there. I am speaking hypothetically. Other than memories, what do I have to show? You almost seem disposable. In these now four years away until March 17, 2019, out of everything that happened, I never turned from God. I did give Him the silent treatment because I honestly had nothing to say, and I didn't want to hear what He had to say. Or if He even had anything to say to me. He hurt my feelings, and I felt that He was cruel at times. Bipolar. You want me to do it; then You don't. Love is mine; then it's not. Music is about to pop off; then it doesn't. It vexed me, but I was not crazy to shelve Him altogether! I do have some sense. I know better.

I just needed to get to know the real Him, not the religious one. For the first time, it was just me and God, one on one, rebuilding our relationship without the distraction of man, the church titles, and everything I thought to be bona fide about my faith. Wow, three years of breaking down my whole being. I almost want to cry right now, thinking about this process. It was hard letting go of what I thought was real all my life and being in the space of "I don't know what is true." "What kind of God are you?" And picking up the Bible? Please. I left it on the floor or in a drawer because every time I opened it; I could not hear His voice. I heard every person that used it to manipulate me, control me, and use me for their gain by it.

I can say I have gained wisdom and understanding. I am spiritually grounded. And I know what I need to do for Dorian. Oh, and the Bible is off the floor now. Lol. I know what I did was from a pure place all those years. But I still wonder, is this the way it is supposed to be? I think not. But that is a much bigger discussion.

SINGING IN THE CHURCH

Will I ever step foot in a church again to sing? I just sang at a church recently. I will sing wherever, whenever, if the environment resonates with where I am personally and spiritually on my path. It does not matter the venue if it resonates with me. If I have peace that it is conducive with where *Dorian* is, book it. I am not anti-church or anti-faith or against people being a part of a church. I believe that everyone is on their designated path. And if they are not, things both seemingly negative and positive are working out in their lives to get them on that path. I am here to create music and offer all the other gifts that are inside of me.

FINISH IT

Check this out. Only a few people from the past question me about attending a church and others say nothing, but they may want to. I already know the scripture reference in their head if they know it. The ones that have taken issue have nothing else to say when they cannot even recall a scripture reference or story I bring up from the Bible. And it's not about the part of the conversation related to church attendance. It may be a random bible story we're discussing, and they will say, "Who is that person or I didn't know that story was in the Bible." See what I'm saying? True story! If I bring up Uzziah, Zacchaeus, or a specific scripture, they have no clue of who that is. But want to debate why I am not sitting up in somebody's church like they are three to four times a week and they don't even know the Bible. And they have been in church just as many years as I was! Knowing scriptures off the top of your head is not a requirement for being a solid Christian. That is not what I am saying.

I also find it interesting that people who judge me and think I need to be in church, the ones who *live* in the church, upon a conversation with them about faith and the scriptures, etc., know little about God. These are the ones that are unaware that certain things are even in the Bible, but one thing they do know is how to do church, their Pastor's favorite anniversary meal, what *she* had on last Sunday, "Giving honor to God...", the order of service, when to shout, etc. But not so much the Bible or even the Creator Himself. But I am the one who needs to be in church? Not mocking, it is just sad and harmful. Just know I am very spiritually grounded. I am not a part of an "institutionalized" church, and I am at peace with that. Some will say, "Bless her heart; she is lost." Nope.

On the contrary, with confidence and humility, I say that I am "more found" and spiritually grounded than most people that attend church. If things change and I end up back in church, then that is the path I am supposed to take again.

A NEW PERSPECTIVE FOR ME

The Answers Always Come

10/28/18 We all have our idea of what church should look and be like, and that is why we choose certain places of worship and why there are attendees at any given place of worship. We believe church should be that way or at least close to it. Or that is all we have known and have a lack of exposure to what else is out there.

Inviting someone to your church is not always the answer. Yes, this may be what some people need, and it has positively impacted many lives. It is easy to tell someone to, "Come to my church; come to my church." But what if there is another spiritual path for them that does not include the four walls of a building but is just as much a God-thing? Why not go to them? Go where they are. Sit with them wherever that may be. Religious people ridiculed Jesus for chillin' with sinners and told Zacchaeus he was coming to his house. Don't get me wrong when I say "sit with *them*" as if there is a picture of what a sinner is. I mean people. Sit with people of all walks, faiths, and races. We are afraid to, or it is uncomfortable. That day, Julius in a sense "came to my house" when he just listened to me. I had a co-worker who offered to send me some excerpts from the Quran. I told her, yes, and she asked for Bible scriptures. We swapped.

I thought it was neat and would have never done that in the past as some teach not to mix faiths or even fellowship with them as it would be a sin. But we eat Sunday dinner or sing on the same praise team with adulterers, liars, porn addicts, etc. But I read the excerpts and watched the videos she sent. To this day, I still have a connection with her, and we laugh together as people. It does not mean that either one of us must convert to connect. But being human feels good. We must be open to all people, and we both realized that what we believe for the most part is not that different. She does not even know how being connected to her was a pivotal part of my spiritual transformation. Thanks, Sarah.

FINISH IT

Transitioning from a Paid Musician

I will say, backing a preacher and playing the "shouting/jubilee" music was never my strong point. I can do it, but it just felt uncomfortable for me to play. I didn't like it. But I know now it had more to do with that not being my path. Kudos to those skilled musicians that can get it in. For my non-church goers who don't know what I mean, I am speaking of the music you play to accompany a preacher during or at the end of his sermon that energizes the atmosphere or brings it home and the music that accompanies a "praise break". Google it if necessary.

Anyway, I can chuckle at it now, but one time I was playing at one of those churches that shout and dance. I mean I was just divorced, a single mom and needed a job. So, the congregation was not picking up what the pastor was putting down, and she wanted me to try and conjure up some music to help her out. And in her displeasure of my accompaniment, with an angry face YELLED at me in front of the whole congregation and said, "I don't want that, I want GOD!!" Well, humiliated, I looked around at the other musicians, and we were all confused. I called her that week and said I would not be returning and to please meet me to give me cash because the church check bounced. There was not much yelling then. I could have been petty and said, "I don't want that. I want a GOOD CHECK!!" Let me stop.

That is where my journey ended in 2012 as far as being paid to play at a church since 1995. I instead became a certified schoolteacher. Although, I did transition to one more church after this until I left the four walls altogether. Even at that church, I opted to attend without musical obligations. I wanted to sit and heal. I told the pastor that I would not be using my gifts this time around. After 20 years of *stuff*, I needed to receive. I didn't want to be on that stage. I needed to heal from a traumatic divorce process, physical abuse, and sexual harassment while in the church from a teen

A NEW PERSPECTIVE FOR ME

into my adulthood, from leaders coming at me inappropriately and an array of things I experienced in the house of faith. I was tired. Eventually, due to a maternity leave situation, I was asked to fill in leading the worship. I agreed under my stipulation that I would not get paid. It was the most freeing time of my church music career. There were no expectations, obligations, or demands. I was becoming free.

There was also the issue of funds being misused in the church, not this church specifically but overall. I just decided that I didn't want to be a part of the problem or be a stumbling block. Remember, I've seen it all. But me choosing not to get paid was not going to fix a deeper issue of mishandling funds in the church abroad. It just gave me peace. There is nothing wrong with being compensated for your time and gifts. Who knows? I may play for a church again that is more fitting for where I am. From 2013 I led and attended a home group for people who still wanted God but was tired of all the other stuff until 2017.

I say to you, **DO YOU**. Embrace your church life just as I have embraced where I am. And if you want to tell me how excellent service was, I will listen and celebrate with you. Focus on you. I see the mask that many churchgoers wear and feel obligated to be at a place that they don't want to be. It breaks my heart to see people week after week walk through those doors, and they feel that they *have* to go to but don't *want* to go. Why are we doing that? Who told you that was right? Why not find a different place or different path that resonates with you? I am sorry, but life is too short to be miserable in any area of life. Free yourself. As for me, I am happy. I am at peace. I am free, and there is no faking that. I am Dorian, and I love her right where she is.

Dealing with Negative People & Opinions

How do I deal with them, you ask? I don't. Overall and 98% of the time, I dismiss, delete, and block from my phone, life, social media, etc. Who has time for that? But there are a few occasions when I do stand up for myself, and as they say, "clap back." If a person chooses to come into my energy space and inbox me something that I didn't ask them about or post on my page a negative comment, they may just be the special winner that day to get blessed. If you allow every person to say what they want, they are sowing seeds and energy with you. I am mindful of my words. So, I keep it classy, and I usually get an apology if they have not cowered and blocked me after posting like a gentleman did today. He sent "GM" (Good Morning) six times and didn't take the clue that I am not interested when I never replied. He decides to go off on me for failing to respond. Ego. Do you think I have time to respond to hundreds of GM's in my inbox?

Of course, people will say don't worry about them, block them. But no. Part of my transformation and being balanced is speaking up for myself sometimes. It is my page/inbox, and just like a person feels they have the right to say what they want on it, I have the choice not to receive it — especially those who claim to be a famous this or that and have contrary advice and comments for me with no credibility. People send me their music all the time. It does not matter where they are in their music journey. I will always give some form of positive feedback, and if they ASK, I will provide them with my opinion. My opinion should not matter either. I know as time goes on, and as I expand my influence, there will be even more of that. Here is my stance...focus on the middle.

Focus on the Middle

I am going to focus on the middle. People like that are low vibrational or have a low way of thinking. There is also the high-minded way of thinking: that I am better than the next, or how can I compete with the next person, get and stay on top, comparing myself to the next, forget where I came from and who was there for me, thinking. Then there is the middle: where I am balanced, I do not suck, but I also am good enough, not better than you but want better for *me*. In the middle I am fulfilling my purpose, influencing others, expanding, making sure my kids are good, making sure my message is pure, focused on what my inner circle is doing, who is too close or not close enough, making sure I am resonating with the people and message that I am putting out. If I focus on that, I will always stay in the middle. We are human, and we can slip either way at any time and need the right people around us.

Negative people, especially strangers, are coming from a place that has nothing to do with me. But they still could receive a strong response from me if warranted. I also believe in the law of sowing and reaping, and that is why I don't waste time on every comment. But I sometimes get convicted when I should say something. So, I do because I know my worth and you are going to know it too if you come at me like that. I am also about building relationships and connections. I will reply, and if they want to fix it, we can stay connected. People make mistakes and do not know they are coming off a certain way. I am pretty sure I have done the same thing. Like one man, a stranger, a *Christian,* sends a message telling me, that I probably should not have done a specific song cover and not pleased with the performance. No greeting, no positive reinforcement first, just those exact words. So, he was the lucky winner that day. The others before him just got deleted. My first thought was to say, "Who in the he** are you?" But I didn't. I told him that he probably should not have come in my inbox along with some other

FINISH IT

things. He said he was sorry and didn't mean to offend and played it off with a kinder comment. There you go. I said, "Forgiven.", and we are still friends on Facebook.

We are here to help each other grow, and I hope that he would think before doing that again to anyone. I could have just told him off and blocked him. But I do believe in connections and growth. You never know who this person might be to you one day. Therefore, I am conscientious about planting fruitful seeds with my actions and my words to everyone. It never fails. Hear me on this. Every time I get one negative comment, either on my page or inbox, within the next few minutes, that same video or post gets slammed with positive comments, likes, shares, and feedback. Every time! Sow good seeds people.

DORIANMARIE; THE MAKING OF

"As I write, I become."

November 2018

11/03/18 Sigh. God, your vision for this project, seems like another bill to me.

11/8/18 Music dad and I had a great conversation prepping for him to come from L.A. Then he calls back asking about my funky energy. He said I just seemed to be off and I was. I was tripping over some songs but also taking it all in. I mean, I was done with music. Here I am preparing for an album and another book when just a year ago, heck, three months ago, I was in a whole other space. I am just… I don't know.

11/9/18 Visited my mom today. (She is not the sentimental type). She asked how everything was going with the music, etc. I told her that I am hoping to get it done by May. After a few seconds, she quietly said, "You will." Sentimental to me.

I love my mother. She is a piece of work, but our family wouldn't work without her. She's that mom that has a paper clip, safety pin, alcohol wipes, cough drops, $.87, a spoon, needle and thread, super glue, peppermints that taste like her perfume, all in that little purse. Whatever we need! And I don't care what stain

FINISH IT

you have on your clothes. After she gets a hold of it, it's coming out. She is sassy but classy. She taught me how to not only make them ends meet but how to look good doing it. You better believe I'm able to do what I do on her shoulders. She still carries me, from the womb to this day.

And my dad thinks because I am his POA that he can just show up at my house with all his paperwork, mail, and phone issues whenever he wants. He can, and he does. It's okay, and I am honored to do it. He is quick to roast me but also quick to maintain my yard. I know that he's been to my house when all the weeds are gone, and it's nicely edged up. He is so sweet. Oh, and by the missing food! Ha! He came by early May when I was at work, and I have Ricola's on my keyboard for my voice. He thought it was regular candy. Nope. He called me later complaining, "What was that mess I ate?" I said, "That's what you get, for always wrapping your lips around my stuff when I'm not here! You need to modify your behavior, sir." Haha! When my mom isn't carrying me on her shoulders, I am riding on his back. He is so supportive and took my first book around to anyone and everyone.

I love you mom and dad and pray that God keeps you here in sound mind so I can repay you and you too can reap the rewards of my labor, although no amount is enough. Talk about the making of *DorianMarie*? It started with these two literally, and it continues as I am still becoming.

11/16/18 Music dad is here from L.A. to lay some songs for the album for four full days!

11/17/18 Day two of studio recording and my heart is full. Yesterday we recorded *Love for You*, and I have no words other than it was fun, beyond what I expected but exactly what I wanted. Today we did a song called *Fallen*. I can feel my heart space opening, healing, and hurting every time I play and sing it.

And this was before Jim came when I was sending him acoustic snippets of the song. I knew then that there was something about it. I get this feeling. One could say I think it is going to be a hit or a huge success. I am sure it will, but it is more than that. It is my truth, and I know someone else's. Maybe it is my current healing process behind the song that makes me feel this way. Or the vulnerability in exposing myself with its message. Unveiling my heart on stage in a church setting was way more comfortable. But even my daughter when I sent her a few snippets of all the songs at once, highlighted *Fallen*. Another person said she had chill bumps when she heard it. Jim had goosebumps and gently said this song is, special. And for some reason that has more of an impact than hearing this song is going to be a hit. We will see guys.

11/18/18 Day three. Today we are going to be working on another new song entitled, *Tell Me*. It is a different kind of song for sure but not sure how to convey that.

Typically, we start creating the song based on the original chords I send, create the beat, etc. But this song was not going well at first. It was not coming together. We spent all day trying to come up with the right sound. Well, he did. When it is going well on a song, I am usually on the floor with my blanket, pillow, talking to myself, doodling, eating, dancing, making noises or running around the house while he is Pro-tooling or something. When I don't like it, I am quiet. I am waiting. Waiting until I hear *it*. But I was falling asleep while he was trying to create from what I sent. I was worried and still. Almost the whole day had passed. Then, "Jim the Jenius" with a J, discards my original ballad sound and starts from scratch and goes left with this crazy sound I had never heard. I sat up, rubbed my eyes, and was like okay, okay. And within 30-40 minutes, he had *it*. A sigh of freakin' relief. I was up, encouraged, and in awe of this guy.

11/21/18 I got a text today. Karimah C. was there when my kids were born and a member of the church where I was the First Lady. She saw it all. We have not spoken in a bit. She was very encouraging today.

When I posted my non-Gospel video, she said it popped up on her YouTube notifications. It was so moving what she said to me. She was honest in her response to my video and was like, "What? Okay, that is not Gospel music." And then she saw another video; she was like, "Okay?" I am laughing as she is telling me this. But she then said, "Well, I'm just glad she is singing again and working on her craft." Man. That made my day! I needed that.

NEW ARTIST

I kid you not when I say I was done with music. Yes, at first back in 2015, I was jaded by all the rejection and what happened with music, the church, and with love. But as of November 2018, something was shifting. I am just taking it all in because it wasn't out of anger in part at God, but out of my twisted thinking that music and love were not for me. And I was cool with that. It was not meant to be. At least I thought.

My Current Music Process

Here is what some singers want to do. Get some songs and get into the studio and put something out. I honor their path. I did that years back as well. But I am choosing a different route this time, or my evolved mind has chosen too. Instead of investing in studio time right now, buying random beats, and trying to "get-er'" done, I am taking my time to develop the sound I want and sit with my songs. Not only that, I am focusing not on the music primarily, but on the message. I have *always* been about the message, with anything that I do. I am attracted to the lyrics first, whether I'm listening to other artists or my work. When I taught music in the church, I stressed learning the lyrics first to the team to connect with the meaning of the song so that one could sing with impact. Because I am a songwriter and delight in the more profound things in life, I am all about the message first and foremost. Vocal flow becomes natural as a result.

On my quest, I am researching my lane. One of my challenges in this process was developing my real voice and perfecting my tone from a churchy sound. In the church you can sing anyway you want in certain places and get away with pretty much anything vocally. You'll get feedback such as, "That's alright baby, just sing for the Lord." There is an intentional sound that I am going for, my authentic sound. And it is not to say that while singing in the church, I just depended on the Spirit while ignoring my technique.

On the contrary, I depended on both. I perfected my voice for the sound in that season. But now I have the task of perfecting my sound for this season in my music career. That means embracing not only the pop sound but the "sensual" sound as well.

This time around is like night and day compared to my last studio recording experience in 2006 and 2013, and even as a teen. Jim told me in the weeks prior that we would be creating the tracks and boy that sounded intimidating to me. I expected like last time, I would sing the song and play the piano for him. Then other musicians would then create the track based on my idea. Oh, but no. This man came in here, made me play on my songs, and we created the track from every bell and whistle. You want me to play the bass line too? (Rolling my eyes). It was new to me, but he explained prior that it is easy to have someone create some beats for an artist and have them just sing over it. That works fine in many cases, and there is nothing wrong with it. I did a rap song a few years back, and that was the case. A producer created a hot track, I "spit some bars" and I still bump *Blazyn* to this day. But today, there is a connection like no other to a song when you, as the artist, can be in the studio or wherever and be a part of the whole process of creating your song.

FINISH IT

Writing for This Album

I also remember telling someone, this time around I want to be involved more in creating the songs, but I didn't think I would be playing on them. That was insecurity and lack of knowledge. For some reason, I had in my mind the machine was going to do it for me. Ha! I recall expressing to a producer who offered to get others to produce my music, that I wanted to meet anyone who would be a part of the album first. I needed to know them, their energy, their spirit to see if I wanted that to transfer on to songs that I paid for in tears, loss, pain, sleepless nights as well as joys and victories. You cannot let everyone have hands on something so precious unless you want to put out something for the sake of it. When you hear this album, every single lyric, I mean every one of them, I lived. You cannot just make a beat for that. What I went through has its designated soundtrack. And when you couple that with someone who understands how a song is supposed to feel and understands you as the artist, the result is powerful. Grateful to have found that in Jim. It saves so much time from having to wait for someone to send you their version of your song only to have them go back and fix something you don't like. I still may in the future sing over an already made track. I am open to anything. But this album is personal. It is my heart wide open, a heart that is still healing in these songs.

People have said God gave you that gift, so use it for Him. But that doesn't mean my music belongs to the church, or it must be faith-based. I have the responsibility as a human being to use those gifts to heal and help all humankind, not just Christians. It's been a process realizing that and that other people felt like my gifts to sing and play belonged to them because they were giving me a paycheck.

That check meant that I must be present and yield my gifts primarily to that organization. I get that. It makes sense to an extent when it is your job/contract. But something was shifting towards the end of my church musicianship. I told myself that I was going to free myself. Now granted, any job that you go to, you are obligated to that place of employment. But for me, working for the church was personal. It connected me to my relationship with God and what I believed in at the time, what I lived by every single day. On a regular corporate job, for the most part, they had me for eight hours, and that was it. But working for the church, I carried home my work, and my work was my faith. After playing at one of the last churches and having the leader scream at me because I was not playing it as she saw fit, I needed to find somewhere I could just sit and not have that responsibility.

11/22/18 I still believe I did nothing wrong in dealing with this person, (keeping this matter private and for my journal only), but after speaking with my cousin about it, I have expanded that thought. She said to me, "This person is not mad at you, but mad at themselves." Geez. That was even more freeing. I spoke my truth, and that is all I can do.

Dorian, This is What You Need to Do

11/22/18 I appreciate a conversation that I had with my cousins, L and J, about the direction I was going to go in as far as signing with a label or staying independent as an artist. Both had contrasting views about what I should do as far as signing with a label or staying independent, but they know me and took the time to hear *me* and what I wanted. It meant a lot to hear their care, and it was funny watching them go back and forth. I felt loved, for real.

Note to people: Before you offer advice, especially unsolicited based on your own experience or knowledge, get to know a person and put on their glasses and see their vision. Everyone has a unique past and history that will map out where they need to go. And everyone is not meant to be a part of it. You may need to offer support financially instead or verbally encourage them. People will

FINISH IT

try to insert themselves and get offended when you gently turn them down. It is essential because certain people were upset when I didn't receive their advice. They had no interest in hearing my vision or what I needed.

11/24/18 Reflecting today: A year ago, I had no idea or desire to do music and music is now present. A year ago, I expected love to be here, and here we are...love is not present...yet.

11/25/18 Still dealing with multiple people trying to tell me what to do with my career. I appreciate the interest that some show, but I find it best to spend time with people and listen to the artist and find out where they want to go, where they have been and where they are now before offering advice. Some were kind while others were downright rude when I refused their advice...again.

Some people assume I don't know what I'm doing because I haven't done it yet or posted it. I am a wise young woman. One thing I look for is a person's resume. You want to manage me, but who have you managed? You think I should stay independent, but you have little to no success yourself doing it. You think I should sign, but who have you worked with and been successful? What major contract have you signed? What mainstream artist have you worked with successfully? When they cannot answer it, they get upset and call me bougie. Hear me. I am not speaking of people who have good intentions and want to share their struggles and setbacks, hoping to steer me from that. Or the ones who are just getting started and need someone to give them a chance. I understand that, and I'm down with that. I am talking about the ones who get upset with me and tell me I am not going to make it because I did not follow their advice. True story. But I'm in love with the delete and block button.

I Am Already There

But here is the deal. Most of these people are advising me from a level that they are on or think I am on or consider me to be on. I am on some whole other stuff. Check this. They see me where I am now vocally, my look, my brand, and assume I plan to stay here. I look at myself as to where I am going. So, I connect with certain people and plan according to where I am going, not where I am. To me, I am already there in mind and spirit; that place I see myself in the future. Therefore, I am listening to people who have worked and touched oxygen space with people like Adele, Lady Gaga, Chris Brown, Rihanna, Quincy Jones, people who have signed contracts with labels and know what they are talking about from experience. And I also listen to people who are successfully independent artists who have never met a celebrity. It is all in the fruit. No, they are not all Christian artists. But they are successful in what they do on a level that is beyond what people are trying to get me to stay on. Their information is not invaluable because they have not worked with celebrities. It is about my path. Then when I tell them funding is what I need most, they go silent or get mad, which lets me know their motives were not about helping me but themselves. Not all of them, just some.

Oh, my goodness. Writing this book in real time? It is wild. So, being back on Facebook for the last three months, I am reconnecting with many from the past. Here goes one. Left me, speechless!

11/28/18 Had lunch with an old acquaintance from when I did music the first time around between the years 2004-2006. He informed me that during that time, someone who was supposed to be close to me was trying to find a way to steal my music right from under me during that time. They wanted to find out how to change parts of the song to get producer credits. This person wanted to know how to copyright the songs under their name too. Songs that they didn't write at all. I came up with the lyrics,

FINISH IT

melody, music, and vocal arrangements. Just speechless. And to know who it was after 14 plus years? Man! There is no statute of limitation with reaping what you sow. Just came back to this on 11/30/18 and I am still processing this one.

I am referring to several faith-based songs that I wrote and recorded for a live album that was never released. Yes, someone, a "Christian" was trying to steal Christian songs from me. Their plan didn't work. I legally had those songs protected and signed by a judge so that person will never be able to touch them. And they wonder why to this day their life is poop, and they are still not fulfilling their dreams. Moving on and up.

11/30/18 I am missing something. I feel stuck on one part of a song, and I need something. I will call some singers I know to write with me. But that's not it. Let's text Jim. Dorian does not like what Jim is going to say. After listening to Jim, I started to see what it was. Yeah, it was partly a lack of confidence that I could write it by myself, but more so I was isolated musically. When I was singing gospel music strictly, I was always surrounded by singers and musicians to sing background vocals, practice music, and increase my skills. Not so with pop music.

Turning Point

I am going to add an entry from December as it relates to and is the solution to the last entry from November.

12/06/18 I am unhappy and frustrated. I am distracted and don't care! I don't have anything to do. I am tired of doing covers, and I want to sing my music. I cannot come up with the pre-chorus or the breaks on none of the songs! My songs are in L.A., and I am irritated with the process. I don't know how to convey this to Jim. It's not impatience or me in a rush. It is something else. I was losing momentum.

DORIANMARIE; THE MAKING OF

I knew what I needed but had no words to describe it. I thought the issue was musical isolation and that was part of it. So, I decided to tell Jim that I wanted to work on some new songs here in Houston with some singers or something. I didn't convey my words right over text to Jim and missed one word causing a misunderstanding and confusion.

Jim was not happy either because I was not happy. That was a tough conversation to have. I didn't like making Jim feel some kind of way. It hurt my heart. After he talked to me about the process, again, he put into words the solution. I needed playback. Meaning, I needed equipment to playback the music we created to practice my vocals, adlibs, etc.... Until then, all I had was my keyboard. And once he took the songs, my babies were gone like my kids leave for 30 days in the summer to their dad's. The house was quiet. I sat there, getting into nonsense and wasting time. That is cool when I have no kids for 30 days, but not when I have a deadline for the album. He said you are frustrated because you need to be creative, and you are like a toddler who needs a toy to keep themselves busy. Spot on! And yes, it is great to be with other singers, but I did not have other singers when I was alone preparing for the worship team as far as learning the vocal parts. So, working alone wasn't the issue. I just needed tools.

So somehow, I need to get a Mac computer, a mic, and a program to play around with my vocals and beats. Problem solved.

MY LOVE LIFE

Did you skip the other sections to be nosey? I'm laughing at you right now, but it's all good. I would do the same thing too! In case you didn't know I've been single for the last ten years since my divorce. I will get into what has been going on the last two years as far as love interests and who if anyone is in the present. But let me give you a backdrop.

Let's see where to start. I had an abortion when I was a teenager, told to get out of a moving car for refusing sex, (it was only about 5 miles per hour) nothing too drastic, pushed down a flight of stairs and hit with a belt like I was a child. I had a shoe thrown at my ankle bone from a jealous ex who found out I had moved on after *he* dumped me and punched in the stomach until I could not breathe to make sure I was not pregnant.

He told me to walk home in the dark or find a ride home, because I wanted to keep myself sexually going forth, had my first heartbreak at 15 when my boyfriend of two years cheated with my bully. I was beaten up in the car while driving down Beltway 8. Looking pretty banged up, no one wanted to get involved. There was the time he poked me in the eye, yes poked, wrestled me to the ground while pregnant, stolen from, abandoned, stalked and while being faithful, I was cheated on in every relationship to date. These adventures took place from the age of 13 to 29 years old. If I've not said it yet, I will NEVER reveal names here or in interviews as that is unnecessary and irrelevant. However, it is my life and my story and telling it heals me. Oh, *he* that I'm referring to is not just one person. I have had six relationships or connections that have impacted the 27 years of my love life in significant ways, and these things took place across the span of them all. I will be 40 this year.

"Some of our pain comes from having expectations and attachments to a person or thing. Open your arms, hands, and mind wholly to God, the Heavens and the entire Universe and release the must be's, have to be's, should be's, what *you* want to be and accept what is meant to be and what will be. It's always better than the ending you planned."

Disclaimer

Now, I have never shared this stuff openly, and only those who were there know it. My mother may see this for the first time or just never told me that she knew. But why share it if I am not going to spill the tea on who they are? Because knowledge of their identity has nothing to do with my healing. Because it's my story, and it's a completion of my healing. It's unfair and unrealistic for a person to hold something in because they feel like they deserved what happened to them. Or you don't want to put dirt, so to speak, on someone else's name. Also, I'm sure anyone reading this has their own story, but my path calls for me to share to the masses or whosoever would read it. It's what happened to me, and if I cannot face my reality, how can I face anything else? How can I be free if I bottle it up, and for what? Holding it in changed me into a certain kind of person I am not called to be. Releasing it and letting it out is also transforming me into another person for the better. I may repeat myself for those who skipped everything else and just came for the love section (smiley face).

"As I navigate this single life, I have learned that a person does not have to be your person or the end all to enjoy the connection. Sometimes there is another purpose for the meeting. I've dealt with this flaw in my past. Now, I go with the flow, learn the lesson without the burden of "Is this the one?" More of, why did I attract you, and what am I to learn? If it turns into something, great. If not, no need to dwell in heartbreak but accept the growth and embrace the new version of whom I've become because of it."

Let's Continue

I've been changing my last name since I was five years old. I just knew my initials would be D.J. from the boy down the street in elementary school or D.D. from the boy at church or D.R. from my first real boyfriend. I married at the age of 21 until I filed for divorce after seven years in 2008 and finalized in 2010. It was a drawn-out tumultuous divorce process, but the best decision for me and the kids. The divorce process took a year and a half. For seven years, I *allowed* because of the church. You know, the "God hates divorce" speech and "what God joins together"…So I prayed and said, "God, I am leaving, and if you never use me to sing, play or speak on a stage again that is fine as long as I can raise my kids and be good with You. I am leaving." I left. I took a stand that last year and said I want to be loved too. I want to know that someone loves me. I want the same energy I had been giving for seven years. Let him find his divine partner, as well. Ironically, when I left, I went on to sing and do more than I ever had, opened for well-known music artists and sang on both local and national television networks.

I no longer wanted to be a crutch or place of comfort for someone else. And as I said before, God didn't join us together. We did. I did. It was convenient, and for the wrong reasons, a means of escape for both parties. It was also necessary for him to find his true happiness as it was not with me. He needed to find joy and tranquility with someone who was a better fit. Sometimes, it's not that someone is just a horrible person. It's just not a match, and the continual discord may reveal that. And that is okay not to be a match. It's challenging for religious people, as I used to be one, to get out of situations that are not for them. We blame Satan and attempt to keep up a pious look while wearing masks in front of people who have nothing to do with our journey. Those same people are probably going through hell in their marriages. Another reason I stayed is that I'm not a quitter. I didn't want to fail at the very thing I wanted all my life. I didn't want to be embarrassed or appear sinful in front of others if I had a failed marriage on my resume. Funny that I called myself praying to God telling *Him* something that He'd been trying to tell me.

It was the strangest thing. We didn't love each other. I knew deep down that it was not the right decision, but I just wanted to be married. I wanted to get out of my mom's house and escape the depression I was dealing with over a previous relationship that ended. It left me confused and broken after a spiritual leader told us to end it, and that was that. And I never knew why. As far as the marriage, I joined us together, and I suffered for it. I recall so many times the Universe was telling and showing me, no! But I did receive God's mercy, grace, and overwhelming love through my two children. He allowed it for me to learn lessons, but I wasn't meant to stay. It worked out for my good in the end, and it is still working out.

Side note: Not sure if you caught this but, the very place I ran from when all of this started is where I ended up running back to, my mom's house. This final time, I left the right way and was blessed to build one of my dream homes.

Dating At 37

So, being married at a young age, I never dated as an adult. In 2010, I was seeing someone for two years, but that ended in 2012 when he said, "I am done with you." I wrote a song about it that year and that song, called *Wings,* is set to be on the next album.

FINISH IT

That is how *Let's Talk it Out* came about. I started writing quotes on Facebook as therapy for myself. People started asking me to expound on the quotes which turned into pages of a book. That brings us to 2013. People have shown interest from time to time, but as my favorite hat said, "Nope." That was the energy I put off after I vowed that I was finished. Technically, I started seeing people as an adult at the age of 37. Why?

From that year until 2017, men and music were not on my radar, nor did I want them to be. I buried them both with no desire to resurrect either one. My albums never came to fruition. And being a relationship person who desired a lifetime partner, I could not make that work either. The men all wanted me to sleep with them, and musically, well they wanted me to sleep with them too to get to the top. If I wanted the attention of a man or to get ahead musically, I would have to give my body to them. That was not an option for me. I even got fired from a church once because I rejected the pastor's advances. So, I thought, screw it all. Music and love are not meant for me. My daughter and I made a pact, which I now know was unhealthy and has been rectified, that she and I would be single for life, and I'd focus on my purse, my education, become a school principal, make more money, raise them, and chill. Oh, and make more money. She was down and loved the dynamic we had along with her brother. Just us three.

I'm telling you I didn't even see men, and I didn't put myself in a position to be approached. I believe it was also a part of my journey to focus on personal accomplishments that I didn't finish in my youth, such as college and becoming a certified teacher. I told my friend that I was now a eunuch, never getting married, or doing the love thing ever again. But now and then, I would mess with my daughter and make comments about men that we would cross in the street, to gross her out and get a good laugh out of it. If I did see a man, I would point out something to her, and she would as most teens, say things like, "Eww, Mom Stop!" Hahaha. I did this all the time, knowing good and well, I would never be interested in another relationship. It happened quite often, until one day, it backfired.

On to the Good Stuff

Guy #6

After a five-year sabbatical, I met someone, #6, in 2017. Boy, did I fight it! When the option came about, I cried and cried for two weeks. I was confused and didn't know how hard my heart was and the need for healing. The Bible study that I was leading met up, and I could not even teach as I just wept and wept. The attendees were staring at me, at each other, as I could not speak. They had never seen me cry, let alone weep, and were ready to fight someone because they thought someone did something to me. I felt like I needed to accept his offer, but what about the vow? The pact? Plus, what's up with all this crying? I hadn't cried in five years! It also meant God, and I would have to talk again. I was cool with sharing and explaining what the Bible said to the ladies, but I wasn't ready to speak to Him about five years ago. But it was time.

Why was my heart betraying me in even considering a date with this dude? I felt out of control and could not say no. I took a risk. But why? I told all of Heaven that I was done with men and love. After all that I have been through with guys, I was for sure I had seared off my heart with vows of "never again." So why? Why did we meet? He came to start the healing process and open me back up to love. He was a mirror to show me things, unfinished business. But this is usually expressed as us pointing out all the things they are doing wrong. When really, they are not hurting us for the most part, but revealing hurt that was already there. My friend jokingly said that I manifested him when playing around with my daughter by fake-flirting or joking about him being my boyfriend. There is

FINISH IT

truth to that. You have what you say. I guess the angels don't get sarcasm when they go to work.

This situation seemed so familiar like the fella who told me he was done with me. It was familiar but different. He opened me up to so many liberties that my limited thinking kept me from enjoying. I became a little bit more of my true self when he came. I wanted to love again because of him. His presence has awakened love and music in me as well as my faith. It has been a lively journey. But after a year and a half, I realized that that was his sole purpose. To open me up. He was a catalyst for something that I didn't know was coming. If it were not for him coming along, I would not have been open to anyone else. He's not the one. I did have my heart set on it, which meant I needed time to heal as it didn't turn out as planned. So, I did just that in August, September, October, November...

December. Whoa. I just met someone else. Not just anyone. Who is he? #7? Stay tuned.

NEW LOVE

What's different about me now is I'm open. Even though there is no one in the picture, my heart is not hard but healing. I know what I want, what I will not put up with, and even more of who I am because of #6. I will say that because all my past attachments are over, I gave details. But this one is new, #7, and I want to protect it, keep it sacred, and see how it will turn out. I will share the process as much as I can. I wrote a song about it on this album called, *Lifetime*. Depending on how things go, it will be a remarkable love story to share later. And if not, that's okay too. But here are a few details.

Okay. Okay, Okay. Giggles. When we met, I was sick with a sinus infection. I looked a mess, messy bun in my hair, no make-up, not an eyebrow in sight. Even if I did, I would have swiped it off as I was rubbing my eyes, head, face, etc., so hard to find relief. I was out in public like this for work. I had no choice. My appearance was his first impression of me. I didn't care because I wasn't there for that. I was open to men at this point, but not that day. I felt horrible. He still chose to engage, bless his heart. I remember him trying to talk to me about something while I was rubbing my face with a tissue. He suggested I go somewhere and lay down, but I couldn't because of work.

But after a few minutes of thought, I did just that. #7 later told me that by the time he looked up, I was gone. When I emerged later from my time laying down and getting some tea, out of 2000 people, we ran into each other serendipitously. Like there is no way we could have done that on our own. Again, I was not there for that, and although I was *open* to men, I wasn't. At that time, my focus was on the book and album. We talked. He was a gentleman. There was an unusual divine connection. It was strange because I don't entertain male strangers. AT ALL! There has to be a mutual friend or something. My friend told me a year ago that I need to be open to meeting someone in public and that it may be a stranger. Umm…no.

I said so I could end up chopped up in pieces in the back of his trunk, then shoved in his freezer until they find me while a modern-day Nancy Grace does a CNN video commentary on how stupid I was to go off with a total stranger? No, ma'am. The only reason #6 had a chance, is because we knew mutual people, he had as much to lose as I did, and though I didn't *know* him, he was not a stranger. I knew where he worked, and he was close to someone I knew. No shade, but I don't want anyone from my past, and I don't want a total stranger. My friend looks at me like, yeah, how is that going to work for you?

But #7 was a total stranger that my soul has already known for a lifetime it seemed. I entertained him with ease. Sigh. Now, this is interesting. I hadn't seen him since I emerged from my nap. It was the last day, and I was putting away my bags in the car after checkout to return inside for the final session. And there he was, parked a few cars away from me, doing the same. We spoke

FINISH IT

and said we'd see each other inside. I was an early bird, so my parking space was on the bottom floor right at the front. Again, out of 2000 participants, and multiple levels for parking, he ends up parking there?

But that's not it. I was parked in that spot for the whole conference as I could not leave, but I had planned to and was looking forward to it. Someone fraudulently used my card the same day I arrived, and the organization charged my card twice, leaving me stuck with no available work funds while they sought to resolve the issue. And after that, I didn't trust using my bank card. So, I had to eat there all those days, compliments of the hotel. However, he was in and out the entire conference, no doubt landing in various parking spots. What are the odds of him parking that close to me on the last day? It was time to go home, and he asked me to go to lunch with some other co-workers, and I did, with a total stranger.

I will admit it, and if he reads this, he will know that while driving behind him, I took a picture of his driver's license in case they found my phone floating in a bayou or the woods. Or if I'm somewhere off in a basement in a random neighborhood where everyone seems happy and I'm down their chained up watching myself on the news as a missing person. My mind can go places, you guys. Anyways, I am also very spiritual and intuitive. I didn't get those vibes at all, and I know myself. I would never have gone had I felt off. My God, who is this man? Not only that, I am hardcore when it comes to who I allow near my heart. Being single for ten years shows that. But how did *he* break through? *Why* did he breakthrough?

NOW, WHAT?

12/03/18 I am blown away. Is this the 7th profound connection? This person just told and showed me everything, and I mean everything, I have wanted to see, hear, and experience my whole life by a man in only two days! A total stranger. But an immediate friend. For the first time in my life, I felt loved, really loved on by a man outside of my father. How can this be? We just met. But the event is over, and we all must go back home. I'm thinking; here we go again with God teasing me. Dangling that carrot. I used to think my kind of person didn't exist. But he does. But now he is gone. Is this some cruel joke from the Universe? Of course, it is. Story of my life.

Here's the thing. It's not like #7 did something totally out of this world or spectacular. He opened the doors; engaged in decent conversation, a perfect gentleman, who asked questions and gave not one derogatory comment or mention about my physique. He didn't even say that I was beautiful. That alone was so refreshing. It was as if he saw *me* first, then what was on the outside. It was a different kind of attraction. Something was pulling us in to talk. I believe he wasn't there looking for anything either.

12/05/18 I cried most of the day reflecting on this connection with a total stranger that I may never see again. That is the only way to explain it. Not love at first sight, not a quickening in my spirit, but a connection. Maybe a love connection. But it was a robust, authentic connection. I am vulnerable, and I like it. He makes me feel like a grown woman and at the same time, a young girl open and ready to be recklessly in love again. I understand him. I want to love him unconditionally, yet I do not even know him, or do I? On a soul level?

Again, he didn't even do anything special as far as textbook things men do when they meet someone for the first time. I paid for my lunch so there'd be no expectations. There's just something about him. It hurts to meet someone so perfect and not be able to have them. It's not ideal because we like the same music, food, both wear contacts/glasses, refuse to iron unless necessary, drink almond milk, deal with allergies, love and sing music, etc. It's perfect because when I saw him, I saw myself. He said I'm the female version of him and vice-versa! If only this, or what if this, or if I had taken this job or moved here, run through our minds. Circumstances and distance keep us as friends.

What I love the most is, he knows nothing about what I do, my book, music, events, and the potential there is for me to go places. So, if it ever became more than a casual meeting at an event, I'd know his motives were pure. He was attracted to me and not who I will be to the world. Check this. I don't know what will become of this two-day unexpected connection, but he has been taking care of me since day one. I looked and felt a mess and didn't care. Neither did he. And he was right, I needed to lay down, and I did feel much better. I told my friend, and I prayed that if I meet someone, I want to meet them now before I do big things musically or with my books so that motives are not an issue.

I don't want them to know anything about what I do. But with social media, people can look you up, which is what is happening now. Men look at my videos and pictures, become infatuated, and come at me based on that. I have received several marriage proposals, and you can only imagine what else has been implanted in my inbox & DMs. They don't know my fears, flaws, insecurities, etc. But in two days we were gifted and allowed to share these things and respond accordingly. I like him a lot, and he likes me as I am. For me, Dorian from the work event and not *"DorianMarie"* from Facebook. His name shall be Twin, for now. More to come.

Growth

I will not say what could be said, but there has been a considerable number of "poopy" things happen to me when it comes to love. People have pooped on my life, left me with the task of cleaning it up without coming back to acknowledge it or apologize. Let me say this, I do not believe this to be as I have taken time to consider all my past connections, but I TRULY apologize to anyone that I have hurt unknowingly. And if possible, I hope to reconcile that

MY LOVE LIFE

and bring healing even without a continued relationship. And that includes any relationship. I had to come back and insert this here as well. On August 28, 2018, the first heartbreak that shifted my view of men at an early age, insisted that I call him after we reconnected when I returned to Facebook that month. I hadn't spoken to him in eight years and have not seen him since 1995. Man, that seems ancient. Anyway, I figured it would be the usual catch-up conversation, but I was given a gift that day. I received the most heartfelt apology from any of my exes. Wait, no other ex has apologized. That's what I'm talking about, in the sense of the need to if possible and if it will not cause more pain, go back and be a vessel of healing. Thank you, C.R.

Do you know what else I've never acknowledged? That in all my relationships, yes all of them from start to finish, I was faithful, loyal, kind, present, an over-giver, and a downright good woman. I've always been marriage material because that is what I've always wanted. It does not mean that all that goodness was always pure. I was still broken even from a young teen. By nature, I was kindhearted, gentle, pure, and soft. But giving that away to people that didn't deserve it was not from a pure loving place. It was from a need for them to validate me, affirm me, and heal me!

I have grown. Yes, I have learned to be in the right now and how to be loved. What Twin did for me in the time we shared, not sure how it will end, has changed my perspective. My problem has always been, what is this? Are we getting married? Did God say you are my husband? I was crazy back then! And even if I didn't ask these questions out loud, boy were they spiraling like a washing machine in my head. I could not enjoy the connection out of fear that I was going to be used, taken advantage of or what not. Wait, I usually was. So, I guess I don't have a point here. Yes, I do. The point is, I needed to go with the flow and when it started to or seemed to not resonate with where I was going or wanted, then it's time to pump the brakes and move around. I wanted to know

FINISH IT

how it would end before I invested. But where is the fun in that? I learned how to have fun. My inner child needed to play. I enjoyed music, but I lacked fun in my life when it came to men.

If Nothing Else

I had fun with Twin! He has shown me what a man is supposed to be but in action. You see it in the movies, hear about it from other people, but Dorian has never had it in person. Let me tell you, he wrote a poem on the spot with my name in it based on our conversation, Face-timed me after we parted, texted and called to make sure I didn't fall asleep driving home, hugged me and a wiped my tears as I shared some details from the past. Oh no, this is not about sex. It was a divine connection, intimacy on a whole other level! If nothing else my prayer was answered that guys like this still exist. I couldn't get the previous ex to even call my phone or FaceTime me and that after seeing each other for over a year. Text only. I didn't have to beg for a picture or to hear his voice. It was only minutes later after he left that I received a photo asking me not to forget him. When I tell you! I had to plead for things like this in the past and never received anything. How could I forget him? He is etched. Tattooed. Engraved. I've always wanted a guy to send me songs, expressing how he felt. Guess what? And I didn't even ask. I looked at my phone like, no. Is this a song dedication? Yes! He texted that I should please listen to his song dedication to me. So hard to let him go. And I only knew him for two days.

There is no shade or offense to any of my past connections. To me, it is redirection that that person is not your person or connection if you must plead and beg all the time. Of course, there may be other things going on, but for my path and my history, it was always about me telling them what I need and want. I received for the moment to start the cycle all over again of not receiving.

MY LOVE LIFE

Disclaimer- Mature Audience Only

Double Time Out: (Kids skip this section, but you probably won't). This time around, I WILL NOT settle for lack of chemistry, lust, or whatever you want to call it. Yes, there will be divine love. For sure. But head to toe, I need and want to be able not to control myself when he walks into the room. I believe it can be that way, and that exists, and the person can still have substance. Especially when you are with your divine counterpart and wait for the total package. Of course, life happens, the daily mundane, duties, routines. And because of that, I need to be physically attracted to you at least, unapologetically. During those times, when we are striving to be on the same page and have those "moments of growth" (disagreeing), I cannot look at you and think man, we're having a challenging moment, and you're not even attractive to me?? No.

I've been there done that. I do not like to use the word ugly to describe people as that is not loving, but you get my point. When that "thing" is there in the relationship, most of the time we don't have to talk about it. Let's just "work it out". I know it exists. Every other time, it was about where they were in their faith or is God saying yes. Not this time. Heaven and I have an agreement. I will know it is Divine not just spiritually but based on my physical response. Period. I must have that this time or I will be a celibate eunuch for life. I am serious. Frustrated for what? I never cared about looks before. But why not? I have settled every time! And I never considered this aspect and have been known to let them come as they are. But this is not the church. I am a woman. I expect arousal and want to like what I see just like men do.

I am a Scorpio, and we rule that area if you know what I mean. And that can help carry us if we are both attractive to each other and "compatible". It can help us revisit that hard moment and bring about unity. Amen? I am dead serious. Therefore, this discussion is a pre-requisite. Trust me. I know when that vibe is there and how

FINISH IT

important it is to choose a person who has the same appetite as you. I will go as far as to say, that will be the FIRST topic of discussion. When I see him, my heart is not the only thing that needs to flutter. We got that. I love you, and you love me. Cool. I know what it is like to feel trapped in a situation where it's just not there. No shots to the exes. They just were not my person, and I was not theirs. I am grateful for this fresh start to get what I finally want and need. Come on somebody!

Okay, let's proceed.

They say it comes when you are not asking for it. But how is it that when I was not looking for it, not expecting it, didn't believe "it" existed or even had it on my radar, I get to experience what I have dreamed about since a little girl and my entire life in two days, only for it to leave? He told me that I said and did everything he ever wanted, and I didn't even know it. It was mutual. But we are two people from two different worlds.

As a rookie dating in this tech era, I was unaware of the expectations of all this new technology and figured, some guys are *text only but talk in person*. But this fella showed me that is not so. I do not have to settle for that. I was like yes, they still exist, but does he exist for me? You may think I am exaggerating, but the Universe showed up and in 48 hours allowed us to be what each other has always wanted. It gave us both hope that it does exist as we both believed it didn't, at least for us. More on this later in my journal entries. The love journey continues.

12/09/18 Photoshoot day! It was cold as heck out there. People may be surprised by some of the pictures, but I love them because they represent who I truly am becoming.

12/10/18 Thinking back to the days when I didn't understand how a Christian could sing non-Christian music. I never judged but could not reconcile it or see how it was okay. However, I saw nothing wrong with it. After posting an Anita Baker cover and another person saying how anointed it was just solidified, even more, I am on the right path. I feel even more spiritually grounded and connected.

12/10/18 You know what? If the connections I have made do not work out, I would like to say I gained friends. That can't apply to everyone, because some people are "you know whats". But if it didn't work out just because it didn't work out, then no need to count that as a loss but hopefully a gain. It is when we think that we've lost something or wanted more from the connection that we feel rejected. And that is when we begin to hurt and complain to our friends that we will never get chosen. When we think of gaining a friend, it makes the letting go and healing process a little easier.

12/11/18 Man! Distractions are real in this season. It happened when I wrote the first book. As soon as I sit down to write, I feel my leg itch. That must be dry skin, so I get up to get the lotion. Is that the doorbell? Let me see. Oh look, the neighbor has new flowers. Let me text her and tell her how nice they are and if I should get that package on their door until they get home. Okay, on the floor, laptop, let's finish this book! As Dorian starts to roll her whole body back and forth from the laptop to the other side of the room and back, and forth and roll. Maybe I need to eat. Focus!!! Sigh.

THE LOOK

Let's go ahead and address this wardrobe situation. I get it. I have always covered up everything based on my convictions growing up in the church. When I came back on Facebook with a wife beater, there were some comments expressed and unexpressed. That is why I'm on the mission I am on as we speak. I have an audience, and it is not the church. My first audience is the person I see in the mirror when I get dressed. If she has peace with it and likes it, that is what she will wear. Back in the church, I never wore a lot of make-up if any, hair was in a low ponytail, modest jewelry, never showed a shoulder, armpit, a full leg, always covered my

FINISH IT

backside, my curves and I hid those toes! That is just what modesty was to me and the directives given. And some things were not fitting, especially if you are on stage leading people in songs of faith. Of course, things have shifted with people now wearing jeans and what not in the church.

I now know that it was more than just me trying to be godly. I was insecure, didn't know myself, afraid of attention from men, and was told not to lead men into sin by our attire as women. I think differently now. When it comes to how I am going to dress as an artist, I will always follow my conviction, preference, and liberty. I am not a Christian artist. I'm just not, and it will take a minute for people to adjust to that and I get it if you have always known me to be one way. I remember hearing about artists, specifically Gospel artists, criticized for what they wore. Well, let me settle your heart now. I am not a Gospel artist, and I will wear what I have peace with, and people that do not like it are not my audience. Do you sit and watch shows that are not interesting to you or offend you? You don't. You are choosing not to sit in that audience for that taping or watch that show. Same applies here.

I am free to wear what is in my heart to wear. Now, my style has always been modest based on my core values as a person, not just a person of faith. So, I am confident that you will not see anything reserved for my future love. But I will not hide what God has given me nor flaunt it in a prideful manner. I am so tired of being stressed about finding clothes to hide in because someone may lust or criticize. Let them lust. That is not my issue, and I let go of that burden. I free myself to be feminine. I free myself to access my sensual side. My friend used to tell me all the time, if she had it like that, she would wear a maxi dress or a fitted dress, things I refused to wear. It was just me living in fear.

Nevertheless, my look will fit my music, my message, and my personality. I love working out, and I used to be a personal trainer. Whether it's my daily life or with music, I would prefer to wear a tracksuit, yoga pants or something like that over getting dolled up. I like to move, dance, and exercise all the time, so I prefer to stay ready wardrobe-wise. You could say I am a tomboy at heart. But I am no longer ashamed of my feminine side, hoping to prevent inappropriate sexual advances that still come even with a dress down to my ankles. From a teen until my 30's, I covered up almost subconsciously, blaming myself for my shape, thanks to my mother. I thought I was causing men to take advantage of or come at me inappropriately. That is not true. I cannot please everyone, and I will not stay in the box that I put myself in. I also have a daughter. I want her to be able to look and listen to any content I put out without being ashamed or embarrassed. So, no worries friends. You will always see classy with a side of "hubba hubba"! **That is Dorian.**

Speaking Of...

I have had a few events in December with some approvals and some "hmmm's" on my choice of attire. It is funny at this point, but once people understand what kind of artist I am, then it will make sense to not hold me to their standards of what I should wear. It's not about denying my faith, but accepting who I am as a person. I lost my identity in religion. And the key word is BALANCE. Oh, how people of faith need to balance all areas of their life.

12/14/18 Hess Club Event- There was something special about this event for me. After speaking to Jim about me as an artist and accepting that I am the artist I see myself as and not who others want me to be, I performed this event with so much ease and comfort. And like he says, "Don't worry about all that other stuff."

12/21/18 Received another random message online about how much anointing is on my voice. That still blesses me as I am singing songs that are not faith based so to speak. Thanks, K.C.

12/21/18 Had the Lasik eye procedure done today. And it was a success!

FINISH IT

Unknown to many, my vision was debilitating, leaving me disabled and almost legally blind. I knew that but felt vulnerable and scared that people would or could take advantage of that if they knew. So, I kept it to myself. My vision has been like this since I started driving as a teen. I was dependent upon glasses and contacts. Not anymore.

12/22/2018 Thinking about when Twin told me that I was **"Every piece of perfect, and if I had to recreate you all over, I would create you just like you are."** *Sigh.*

Mind you, when we met, I was ALL natural and looking rough. And Twin is the only man that I have connected with that has seen *me*. Just me. And he liked it a lot. I guess.

What Kind of Artist Are You?

I'm making music that no one is exempt from hearing. I used to make music that was only for Christians. Now I make music for any and every one. That's what I love the most about this new path. If you are in a relationship with anyone, family, friendships, or romantic relationships, my music is for you. If you happen to be a Christian, you also can be touched by my music.

Take me out of the box labeled, "Christian making love music for Christians." I am not a gospel artist making love music for Christians. I am an artist making music for whosoever will listen. I create music for people of all faiths to listen to that will nurture all their relationships. For those who do wear that label, there's nothing wrong with that if that's what they want. That's why my album is called *My Other Playlist*. The whole point of me pursuing my new path is to get out of a box that I was put in.

15 MINUTES

12/26/18 Today marks the first anniversary of my aunt Gladys's passing. Rest in Heaven Auntie.

Let's pause for a second. I have never seen anyone leave the earth up close until December 26, 2017. Even a year later, to see someone's last 15 minutes on earth. I am still processing the impact this had on me. Candice, her daughter, posted a video about the power of 15 minutes in honor of her mom because that is how long it took once the machine was unplugged, and she left this earth to rest.

The doctor said it would be less than an hour. It was not many people in the room other than her children, another cousin, and me. It was unexpected as she is the youngest Aunt out of all the siblings. After being in a coma for weeks, the family decided to let her go. She was tired, and just lost her son unexpectedly two years ago (rest in heaven, Rodney). It was a week of sharing fun memories, tears, shock, questions, decisions, and all this right before Christmas. I remember calling another aunt who was out of state and putting her on speaker phone, placing the phone to my aunt Gladys' ear, leaving the room so she could speak to her spirit as her body was unresponsive. The most powerful thing I have ever experienced outside of childbirth happened next.

I sat at the foot of the bed, watching the nurses and the doctor do what they do as we prepared to say goodbye. I remember the monitor for her heart beating at around the number 50. Once the machines were off, her children gathered around the bed to say

FINISH IT

goodbye. I tell you the number 50 started to climb slowly to 85 as if she could hear our voices as each one spoke words of love, comfort, peace, their farewells and to give us time. I believe she listened to every word. We each had the chance to say goodbye, touch her and love on her. It was calm and even a few giggles because my cousin Candice had no filter and provided much comic relief. I remember how in those weeks before they said the machines would react whenever Candice was in rare form. As if my aunt was saying, "Shut-up Candice!" Lol.

But soon, that 15-minute window started to close. And just as those numbers went up slowly, they dropped quickly. For some reason, I could not stop watching the machine as the numbers dropped. I remember hearing the farewells speed up in the background, but my eyes fixated on the numbers. My heart started beating fast. I was scared, sad, grateful to be there, confused as to why I was, all over the place. But it was not about me, so I held it in. The numbers were skipping, and I had each number memorized to zero for days after. She was finally at rest. I didn't sleep or speak for days about it. I couldn't. Preoccupied with the music, getting the program in order, planning the service, going over the songs, and keeping family informed, kept me distracted. I was too busy to process the experience and grieve. Eventually, I did. I'll never be the same, and I was so honored to play a role. And she could cook too! Love you, Auntie.

MY ISSUES WITH LOVE

"The Universe is acting <u>now</u> on your behalf based on a greater future for you."

Though I carried the fear of all that bad stuff happening again and decided to remain single, I still do not believe that all guys cheat or beat. If they all cheated or were abusive, there was something in me that attracted that type of person and allowed it. It does not excuse or justify it, and it was *not* my fault. But it is the truth. And the only way to not cut and paste from my past to my future or present is to acknowledge that. I have transformed. I am not that same girl.

My issues in love were my issues with me. I could not get it right. But I look at myself today, and I am so glad that I am not officially with anyone because I had no idea that I would be so different from who I was a few years ago. I am grateful for this time to expand and grow into who I want to be so that my person can be my equal and match my vibration. I think if I had partnered with someone three or four years ago, that connection would have matched the other version of me and not the real me. I am settling into this Dorian, and I like her.

Just like we can lose our identity in marriage, we can do the same in religion/church. It happened to me in both cases. We get lost in duties, titles, and distracted from the purpose of our faith. We neglect to nurture ourselves as human beings. It is prevalent to be the best version and most authentic you <u>before</u> you come into

FINISH IT

a union, so they can accept you as you are, and you can attract the best match for you.

I want to think that my past relationships didn't work because I would expand or evolve in my thinking that that person would not have. Or they would expand in a way not conducive to my path. Therefore, the relationship would not have worked. Again, it is not that either person is a wicked person. It was just about my future. So, I no longer take the break-ups personal. It's about my future.

I Love Dorian

There was a time that positively describing myself counted as being vain. But to describe yourself is to know yourself, if you are willing to be honest. People do it all the time. They acknowledge negative traits that they need to work on, so what issue is there in recognizing the positive traits? An honest evaluation of yourself shows where there may be an imbalance. If you are that person who will shank somebody without a thought and knows that you are aggressive, you also know the possible consequences of uncontrollable wrath. But equally so, me being an over-giver, over-lover, and one who self-sacrificed, realize the effects to that as well. There must be a balance. I am still that real one that can overwhelm you with passion, treats, and affection, whether friendly or romantically. But know I am just as much that real one with a sharp tongue. One that will speak words of truth that can trigger you or cause you to either transform into something better or words that can make you struggle for the rest of your life. But people are not used to that and rarely see it. I rarely attract that energy in my life as I do not put that energy out. But it is there when I need it. Don't let this smile fool you. I also need people in my life to support and sharpen me as well.

I'm sure that what I'm saying is not new to most, but it will resonate if you have been there or are there currently. But every, and I mean every, connection and relationship that enters your life is a reflection, to show you where you are. It can be a test to see if you have learned the lessons. We are mirrors for one another.

Dorian the Caterer

All my life I have catered to people. I looked over all my connections, the romantic ones, friendships, at work, and especially when I was in the church. It was always about what I had to offer. I never questioned what the other side or party had to offer. That was never on the table or something that I wanted to challenge. I just gave. But now that I am about to turn 40, this is the first time in my life I have asked what the other party has to offer me, so that this can be a balanced relationship, friendship, work-ship, music-ship, situation-ship, etc....I may not ask it out loud but mentally I'm observing if this is balanced. Yes, there are connections where one party may give more for a season and a reason. But continual depletion, because others are not depositing back into you, is not okay.

Man, I used to let people run over me and not speak up for myself because I didn't feel worthy. No one ever said I was unworthy. I just compared myself to others. As a teen, the other girls wore make-up, the latest trends in fashion and hair. I was bland, dull, country, and sheltered. I had/have never been to a club or experimented with drugs. And when I had a boyfriend, it was always for two years or more. So not much experience with the boys or drinking. Quite naïve, I would say. One time a group of teens from the church asked me to go to this club called *Jamaica, Jamaica*. I was so scared. They talked me into it all day, but I had no peace about it. I eventually agreed and got dressed. I had on a long sleeve multi-colored wool shirt, black non-tight jeans, calf socks, and loafers. I thought it was okay. Boy did they look disgusted when I came to the car, but that was all I had. When we got there, we stood in the line, but I could not go in. I felt so bad because they were fussing at me for having to drive me all the way home.

FINISH IT

Well, Will You At Least Have a Drink?

I only drank once as a teen and didn't drink again until I was 37. This same group of teens told me to come to a party at a house. I agreed thinking it was a family get together type of gig…so green and naïve. There were no parents — only a couple of teenagers and a lot of alcohol. I saw a couple of people go into rooms and I was terrified. Again, wanting to feel included, I was coerced by my then boyfriend and the rest of them to drink a gold drink with gold flakes in it. Cliché as it is, I didn't want to seem uncool. Everything in me told me, no. But I did it anyway. Everyone else was drunk and seemed happy and giddy, so why not?

After only a few of those, being a first-time drinker, I was drunk. I remember a guy trying to get me to go into a room with him. He was not my boyfriend. It was his friend. Of course, I had little to no control, but I remember it like yesterday. He kept telling me that I needed to go lay down, and there was a room right around the corner. I can see the layout of the house. I kept declining while looking for my boyfriend. Eventually, I ended up in the room, and he laid me down on my back. I knew he was wrong for this, but I was too weak to call out. I was hoping this was not about to happen. He was physically stronger than me, and I was in a daze. As soon as he got on top of me, my boyfriend did come in on time and scolded him. It was a Saturday night, and I woke up in that house and rushed home with another girl from the party to get dressed for church, to play and lead the choir. We hit a ditch because I was tired and hungover but made it safely. That was in the late '90s, and I never took another drink until 2017.

I was traumatized and feared that I would lose control or be taken advantage of again. I was okay with not being a drinker. But I still always felt left out and could not relate to others when we ate or hung out, even as an adult. I kid you not. Everybody, I mean everybody around me was drinkers, such as my family, friends, and co-workers. For some reason, I faced that fear when an acquaintance asked if I drank. I said no. They asked me why. No one had ever asked me why. I cannot believe that I am about to dig this up and talk about it. It was time. So, they introduced me to a small amount. I think I told them that was enough before it hit the bottom of the cup. It was more about overcoming the fear because I wasn't fond of the taste. So, in 2017, whenever I did taste something, I was surrounded by friends and family. It felt good to be free from that fear and trauma. Still not much of a drinker, but if I go out with friends and I want to have a drink socially, I order my little rookie drink, and that's all I need. Or I can decline, primarily to protect my voice. And I always have that one cousin that gives me that look as to say, "You can't have that, and you fasho ain't ready for that."

12/27/18 Met a fellow music mate. One of those right on time connections where both share their journey and confirm that where we are and where we are going is the right path. Our personal and music journey's mirror each other. We spoke of the shift in the type of music we desired to do being people of faith and the challenges that come with that. We both needed that conversation. Thanks, D.T. aka... (inside joke).

12/28/18 Why do boys have to like MY daughter? And why does she have to care? Sigh, I do not have time for this.

PAST PERSONALITY FLAWS

Here's the deal. My previous book, *Let's Talk it Out* (available now online or at a future book signing event near you (smiley face)), was an anthem of healing for me because I didn't talk. I didn't know what to say when I needed to stand up for myself. Sometimes I was unaware that an unfair situation was even taking place, all in the name of me being a good Christian. *Allowing* people to hurt you is not what I am advocating when I promote that word. I have always allowed people to be who they are and receive what they needed from me. But it was unrequited, imbalanced and unequal

FINISH IT

in the give and take. I had an issue with accepting just any kind of treatment. As if I was helpless in how people treated me and how the dynamic of a relationship was going. I was always getting the short end of the stick.

I mean from simple things like the other day. I was in the store, and I looked at the grocery store app, and it said that a carton of eggs was on sale for $.99. So, I go to the register, and they rang up for $3.19. I proceeded to tell the cashier and show her my phone where it says $.99 with a valid coupon date. She said, "Oh, but its $3.19 on the screen." I said, "Okay, well, let's pick up the newspaper ad that's laying there by your register and see where it says $.99, as well as on my phone." "But it's not ringing up like that," she states. The truth is, I had a full carton of eggs at home and did not need them. So, I realized it was a lesson after the fact. The old Dorian would have looked back at the line, saw those ten people waiting and said, "That's okay; I'll just put them back or pay the $3.19."

So, she pulls out a coupon in her drawer, and it says the eggs are $.99. The cashier scans it, and it still doesn't work. I'm still standing there as she goes away to tell her manager and asks her manager for the override key. She comes back with the key and asks if I still wanted the eggs. I said, yes. She looked relieved until I said, "But not for $3.19." with a straight face. Looking peeved, she thought it was over — another attempt and still $3.19. I said, "Again ma'am, my phone, your paper and the coupon in your hand, says $.99." This dance went on for four minutes. She asked me again if I still wanted the eggs and I said yes. She's like, "Great." Because it would make the line go down, she will not have to do another override, and it's more comfortable for *her*. But I am not paying $3.19.

The young lady stands there looking at me, and I stand there looking at her, with this long line when all she had to do was honor it and put it in manually. I know, I was a cashier just like her before.

Matter of fact, I opened that store as a teen cashier and put up the shelves and did the floors that she was standing on. And, I'm sure high-butt Randall's can take one for the team seeing that three sources said $.99 and there was a valid expiration date! It was a quiet four-minute exchange, nothing hostile as that would have been unnecessary. I quietly stood my ground and stated the facts, no emotion needed. Plus, I shop there weekly, high prices and all, more so for the convenient location.

You may not think it's a big deal, but this was a massive test for me, and many tests took place that week like this. The old unhealed me let people walk all over me for their comfort in both severe and trivial matters in life. I used to be afraid to ask for ketchup in the drive-thru for goodness sake, knowing good and well that ketchup made the fries for me. There I was, eating dry fries all the time when I *know* I asked for it with my order. Walking away from something that I wanted, deserved and earned because the other party may be uncomfortable, is a prime example of how I used to be in my relationships, in the church, with friends, etc. If there were an injustice, I would suppress what I wanted in favor of their comfort. Well, I walked out of that store with my eggs for my egg whites and oatmeal the next day.

But most importantly, I felt good about myself. In the past, I would feel guilty and vexed as if I deserved not to get what I wanted — a twisted unhealed mindset. And guess what? I didn't have to get ignorant or loud. I kept a smile on my face and stated the facts. I was very kind, and when she handed me the bag, I thanked her and walked away. It was the principle. If you compromise in small things, you will compromise yourself in grander things.

Fair Exchange

The main issue I had in all relationships was giving people space to be, to tell me their problems, their feelings, and I was the perfect

FINISH IT

listener. People would hit me up with, "I need to talk to you." "Call me, I need some encouragement," and so forth. Is that okay sometimes? Yes, maybe, and it depends. It happened 95% of the time. But what about me? It was rare that a call was totally about me or even over half the conversation. The conversation may start off talking about me for about 13 minutes, and then the other 149 minutes would be about that person. Those numbers are accurate. I documented it as I noticed patterns. And this was ALL the time. I am an empath, so that puts me in a position to be a good listener and easy to observe another person's energy. I now have boundaries.

Another issue was not being able to stand in my truth because I didn't know my truth or how to express it without fear of them leaving or hurting their feelings. But boy, the day I stood in my truth, people ran/ghosted me, became defensive, became upset and left the building. You would think the main issue was what I said or how I said it. Nope. The problem was, after all that time that I invested in these people, I realized there was never space for me to share my truth or my feelings. It was not about me telling them how I felt, and they should comply. It was that there was no space for me to tell them how I felt period and receive meaningful feedback. There was no place for me to be a real friend to them and vice versa.

01/03/19 The young man from my teenage days that I received an apology from back in August, reached out to me again after seeing some activity online and wanted to share kind words of encouragement. I thought when he apologized the first time, that my healing was complete from when he broke my heart and set me on a course of insecurity. His actions were an attack on my sense of self. But today, I didn't just listen to his apology because he apologized again in depth. This time I shared how his actions impacted me and their effects. I was hurt. Broken. And he never knew what it did to me. Now, my healing is complete concerning that matter.

People Wanting Your Time

01/03/19 Wow. Ego. Another one blocked because I refuse to accept their advances musically and romantically. It is ego when a person, me, kindly tells you more than once that I will get back with you when my projects are complete. They still proceed to send these long defensive replies in my DM's on both of their pages, instead of respecting where I'm at and going on their merry way. Irritating. Blocked.

I do not like it when people come at me romantically and then want to do shows and music together. That is a turn off to me and unprofessional. Motives are unclear, and it is distracting.

First, it's all about the connection when it comes to who I will work with on any project. Everyone wants to make music with you or whatever your craft is, especially when there's something mutually beneficial. But I go off vibes, discernment, and wisdom. Second, understandably people will request that you show them how you did what you did. I get that, and I've always been willing to share whatever I know. No one taught me anything about writing a book. I learned and did it myself as well as many other things. Because my time is valuable, I require compensation for those hours I mentor people in writing, music, when I had my credit repair business and fitness. I will tell you why.

I used to spend hours coaching people and sharing all the tools I used for my various crafts for free. Only to find out, three months later, a year or even three years later, that they are still in the same predicament or worse before I gave the advice and resources. Then, they come back and ask me to help them all over again with the same information. There are other times I feel a "give it away for free" spirit. But for the most part, I charge, because if they do nothing, at least I don't feel taken advantage of or mismanagement of my time. That is the time that I could've spent working on my craft. But if compensated, I can use that to fund my lifework, and if they do nothing with what I taught them, that is on them. There is nothing I value more than my time, whether business, pleasure or doing absolutely nothing. Laying around doing nothing is sacred to me.

So, if you want to glean from someone, at least offer to compensate and be prepared to do so, even if they decline your gift. And the exchange doesn't always have to be monetary. Maybe you're a talented hairstylist and are unable to offer money in this season for someone's time or tips on how they opened their business. Offer to babysit if you know the person. Say you're good at making videos for social media and you know someone very influential. Create great videos to promote their page in exchange for sound wisdom while simultaneously getting exposure to your talent. Sow into yourself. Don't be a leech. Let there be an energy exchange so both parties can benefit.

"I made life easier for others while forgetting to love myself."

01/05/19 Self-Mastery. When singles come to me and complain about being single, I share this. I told someone today that I tend to think that self-mastery is critical. Meaning, master those out of control emotions. I've been there and still working on it. I ask, why does the person show up when you could care less? Or when you have gotten over the fact that you are single, and have finally become content with just living your best life? Because you have mastered your emotions, fears, self-esteem issues, and the feeling that something must be "wrong with me." You may have your moments, but mastering yourself puts you in your power. And that my friend makes you attractive. That whiny, self-pity, resentful energy repels your potential mate. Find and use the tools and resources to overcome pining over someone who will not show up until you do the work.

Speaking of Energy Exchange

I never knew there was no space to share my pain until I did, and no one was there for me.

When I was a good listener, gave a sound word, or boosted that ego, I was worth their time. But as soon as I expected the same in return...crickets. Even if they didn't agree with what I said, I expected them to at least acknowledge my feelings. People see me as strong, independent, and in my power, and it is so. But like Twyla Paris says, "Deep inside this armor, a warrior is a child." You may not know how to fix what I'm dealing with, or you may not even agree, but acknowledge that I am "feeling some kind of way."

Dear one, there is no need to entertain anything or anyone that is not giving you what you want or need. In other words, if it is not serving you, drop it. You can create what you see in your heart and mind. It may take time to transition out of it, and it may be a process. When I began to use my logic over my emotions, that's when I started winning. It applies to all areas of life. When I was 24/7 in the church, it was a given to serve God and then serve others. But they didn't emphasize balance. I look at where I am now, and these last three years, I have served myself first. It took over 20 years to get here. It feels great and makes me even *more* effective when serving others. It's no different than putting on your mask first if a plane goes down.

01/06/19 I told my friend today that I've felt and still feel like a therapeutic couch that people come and lay their head on. But it's rare that someone will ask me, "How does that make you feel?" I told her this bothers me. I'm not referring to my clients and my lifework, but people who said they were my friend. I asked her if I was the common denominator, maybe I'm the issue. Am I not intriguing enough for people to ask about my life or do people perceive me as one who does not want or need the same in return? When I listen to people, I am active, I am all in, giving feedback, nods, purposeful questions, and solutions. But it seems like people look to me for answers only or to cut me off to interject their issue.

I'm not exaggerating when I tell you from a teen to adulthood, I did nothing but serve others, and most of the time, it was unreciprocated. And this is no one's fault but mine. And it is not so much a fault but an observation and reality. I didn't know any better. In 2015, I just woke up. And then I saw that I had nothing to show for it tangibly. But I know that God does not forget our labor of love and the place of purity in which we serve. I never said no or took off as a church musician, at times when I should have. We do it on our 9-5's, don't we? I didn't want to let the church or God down, people-pleasing while needs went unmet.

My children couldn't be involved with outside activities. I had to leave my own child's birthday party to play for a Saturday service. I can only remember one date night that my ex-husband and I had while in the church or when I was the First Lady, and our car didn't even make it out of the neighborhood because something came up. And we wonder why most kids, spouses, specifically men, end up resenting the church and God. Parents and spouses become church addicts. It is another reason why divorce is common in the church and why parents struggle to have a relationship with their teenagers. Yes, we can be addicted to church if we do not master or cultivate balance.

MORE ON THE LOVE FRONT

I've always been the recipient of heartbreak. *I just realized that my heart broke in 1995, and it wasn't until last year when I met Twin, that true healing arrived. He came to heal me.* Anyways, as far as dating or getting to know someone, I used to think that if you just met someone and you are spending time with them, you are cheating if you entertain someone else at the same time. I'm just a one-person gal. Man, this is so different for me but good for me. It is now January 2019, and it has been six months since I have decided that I need to stop being stuck on one person all the time and get to know multiple people platonically without wondering if we will marry or if they are here to use me. I was extreme, and it had to be one or the other, no in between. You find someone, start praying if he or she is the one lest you fall into sin. That is indoctrination at its best. But I think it is healthier for me considering my past that I entertain the male energy on a friendship level first, whether it be one or three.

So, a few months ago, I'd say in the Fall, I went on a couple of lunch and dinner dates, outings just for the sake of enjoying myself with a nice gentleman, some for business, and some platonically. Although, I knew they were crushing on your girl. I've had one or two online conversations with the non-crazy ones who do not go ballistic in my inbox when I show no interest. But I was looking for a *connection*. I did find it a month ago, as I spoke of him earlier and boy, has he shaken me up. I can say he has my heart. But he's not even here.

*"I don't have to ask you for what I want.
Your soul already knows because we are one."*

Gentlemen Callers

Here is the kicker, I conversed with these guys on Facebook or text with no expectations. I've healed that part of me that says, "It must be meant to be because we are talking or attracted to each other." "Oh yeah, he is a Christian, so it must be, right?" And I've also healed that part that thinks that they are here to use me and break my heart. I'm just here going with the flow. I watch them flow in and out with no attachments. It is healthy for *me*. I attached myself in the past to the first thing which always turned out to not be the best thing. So, when they roll out now, there is no praying them back. If it is meant to be, it will be. The process is much quicker now because my energy is well refined, and if we are not clicking, I clock out.

Man, I have grown to be able to handle this. Usually, the exchanges last about a day or two because honestly, since I decided to do this book and album that is my focus. And if there is no connection or purpose, I do not waste time. If people only knew the obstacles I have overcome, they would understand this season of focus. The goal is to have this done by May; then I can come out and play.

Then there is Twin. Though we are apart, he is here, and I am there. I feel his support, his friendship. It is not time for me to be in anything serious right now because I need this season. Maybe the timing is off. It cannot go any further than our meeting. But I believe he was sent into my life to keep my heart from distractions and to restore my hope not just in true love, but that you can have what your heart desires. I spoke earlier about living an uninspired life during that marital season. When and ever since I met Twin, I've been inspired! I've always worked out, being a personal trainer as my first teen job, returned to my healthy eating habits for the last ten years, and live a health-conscious lifestyle in general. But just the memory of him gets me off the floor fast and to the gym. The thought of him makes me want to be a better version of myself. When I was in his presence those two days, I wanted to write more in my book and work on my album when I got home. He inspired me! On my own, I motivate myself well. But he pushes me further than I would typically go, simply because he exists, and we connected. I want that for life. And I will not settle for not having it.

When They Return

I have had exes return who were able to find me on Facebook. I spoke of the one who apologized. The rest, for the most part, are captivated with what they see online as they do not know me, the new me. Long gone is that easily duped middle school, high school, church girl who was taken advantage of and used. I'm telling you! Twin set the standard of how a man should treat me. I told one ex, who respectfully understood, that if I went back with any of my exes including him, it would be a win for them, not for me. I feel like anyone from the past that would want to come at the highest height of my life so far, especially if they didn't treat me right which none did, how is that a sweet ending to my love story? It would be different if I felt like someone was the one that got away. I am finding out that I am that for them, but they are not that for me. I am amazed that there is no one from the past that I can consider the one that got away. I know I didn't want Twin to get away.

FINISH IT

They Just Walked Away

If you are the type of person that holds people accountable, know that some people are just not ready to be in your life because you will not allow them to sit back and do nothing with theirs. Even family. If what I said was not true, ignore it, live your best life, agree to disagree, and let's have lunch. But to ignore, walk away and end the connection abruptly after I speak my truth about things I see in your life when you were the one that approached me about it? No, I was a mirror, and you didn't like your reflection. I get it, having to go through facing myself as well. It explains why I take full responsibility for my previous marriage and divorce. I chose that, and therefore, I chose and accepted everything I went through in its entirety.

Next time around, my family and friends need not worry or threaten my future love about hurting me and giving him the side eye. That's offensive to me. I'm sure some will, but if I attract my past into my life again, I am the one who needs a butt-whippin', because our partners reflect who we are. As if I would bring another person like that into my life, my home, around my kids, after all this time of healing, loss and restoration and years of growth. I'm not the same person, and I will attract that which is of my highest good only. I hope that when I present my person into my world, the perception and response will be one of, "If she chose him, he must be quality, has her best interest at heart and is her divine counterpart. We love him already." But people will think what they want rather than evaluate where I am, what I've done in my life to this point and not pay attention to who I am now.

I have never been drawn to do crack or have the tendency to steal or lie. So, you cannot tempt me with that. I've worked intensely on my areas of weakness, and I have gone through enough pain and rebuilding not to choose that old path again. People can change, and it can be permanent. Especially when you've gone through

MORE ON THE LOVE FRONT

enough loss. Yes, we are human and can fall anytime, but you get the point, I hope. My future Mr. is the one my family needs to pray for (smiley face) because I am a piece of work. A beautiful work that is still in progress. I know what I deserve now, and since I am willing to give what I know he deserves, I expect nothing less. He will see that he is loved and that he has all of me. I believe I will and better get the same in return. That's all.

01/09/19 Jim talks to me about the snakes and how people will base your availability to them according to what is going on in their life. They feel like they have time to chill, and so should you. That is not the case when you are a single mom running her own business, writing a book, and doing an album at the same time. Because they are not on their mission, they seek your time and energy to take you off yours, intentionally and unintentionally.

01/12/19 I thought I was strong before, but after the recent changes in business and love, I have accessed even more inner strength to carry me through. It hurts. When I heal, sometimes I need to be alone lest I bleed on someone. I must be quiet and refrain from speaking.

01/13/19 Facing a fear today. Will I be fulfilled? So tired of "almost him." Each time, he looks more and more of what I want, but there is always an obstacle, a catch, a dangling carrot...I'm just bleeding right now. Tomorrow, my faith will arise again.

01/14/19 Okay, I will still believe. Change of perspective. I do not consider this a loss in love, but a temporary 'pause in action' to bring about a better outcome for all parties involved. I look forward to what will and could be in the future. Be optimistic. If I experienced him, and it was better than the one before, what is to come will be a thousand times better. My perspective is healing.

01/15/19 Fine. You win Jim. He bugs me even when he does not even know it. I am at my keyboard, and I am bored. Why? Because Jim told me to get off the keyboard, get out of my comfort zone, and go into the living room, and sing without it. So, I'm up.

A Little More About Twin

01/15/19 Reflecting on Twin. He showed me what kind of man I want and my soul desires. I was able to express myself without him ghosting me or ignoring me. He was a friend. Twin showed me that this rare breed of men still exists. One who stands in his divine masculinity but is in touch with his emotions.

01/23/19 Through our brief friendship, Twin, *came to resurrect and reconstruct that which other people tried to destroy in me;* These were his words to me. He triggered me into healing. I am sure I did the same for him. I learned to trust in love again fully. And to trust in God *for* love again. Even if Twin was or is not for me, the fact that we met and he is the perfect counterpart, says that love remembers me, and my heart's desire is within reach.

01/29/19 Man, another round of emotional healing today. It just comes out of nowhere. Just when you think you have cleared all the layers from the past.

01/31/19 Twin brings me comfort. Reflecting on the time, he sang to me about not worrying. His voice is so soothing. I am so thankful to have met him.

FOX & I LEARNED THE HARD WAY

Something I am thinking about today. We can 'what if' all day long. What if I had of left sooner? I stayed so long and became someone I was not. I was a pretender instead of being authentic. Fox wouldn't have done the things he did concerning *her* if he'd honored his heart from the start. Whether there was a physical betrayal, I have no proof, but I know his heart was far from me along with some other incidents to confirm that. I genuinely believe that he didn't enjoy being in conflict or treating me that way. I know. I lived with him, and I saw it on his face and felt it through his absence. People may criticize and say I should've walked away when he was going back and forth with the ring. But he was not the same person before the marriage as he was inside of the marriage. Despite my lust for marriage and his lust for ministry, I saw a man who genuinely was seeking to hear God and choose the best path for himself. I watched him pray; we prayed together. I think once in the marriage and reality set in, that this was not it, it turned us into different people.

I wouldn't have married a monster, and that was not the energy he was in before the marriage. He was not a player. He was sweet and gentle. It's weird, but although I was the recipient of that pain caused by his actions, my heart goes out to *that* man with compassion. He was searching and trying to reconcile what was in his heart and the pressure to have a wife for ministry…one he barely knew.

FINISH IT

Because in the beginning, he wholeheartedly was trying to please God and choose the right path. I believe that. That's why I stated I would leave out the details of the seven years. That was the effect of not being with the right person. It's not to say that she *was*. If she was his divine partner, then heck, maybe he was unfaithful to her by choosing me; if that's where his heart was. Honestly, none of us should've gotten married, period.

We were too young and undoubtedly not ready. The answer was more on the lines of wait, not who. (That's what I mean by religion pushing people to marry sooner than later for the wrong reasons). Talk about looking miserable, terrified, and lost at the courthouse. Not me, him. Bless his heart. Come to think of it, the four people that were a part of that day, all appeared stoic with painted smiles. I saw it but ignored it. We'll be alright guys, I was thinking. They knew! Marrying him was not right. Deep down, behind my smile, I knew it too.

I'm telling you. We are mirrors, and you will attract your reflection. And if you need to learn a lesson because you won't heal or deal with your issue, the Universe will allow you to indulge in your desire until it almost kills you and you surrender. We both operated in lust, which cost us. I wanted marriage. He wanted a ministry. But it wasn't time and nor was it with the right people. So instead of waiting, we followed our lust. As I sit and reflect on some things that both she and Pierre expressed, it's highly possible that the people we *really* wanted were not ready for what we wanted. We weren't even ready ourselves. Wow. It's just now hitting me, some specific conversations from the other parties.

The way to be authentic is to honor your desires. And that is with anything! You start to slack on the job, decline on work ethics, and not care as much anymore. That could be a sign; it's time to leave. But since we are speaking about love, honor your desires. When you don't, you become someone you don't want to be. It's one, I said one, reason people are unfaithful. They are afraid to honor what they want for various reasons. People shock themselves when they find themselves, lying, sneaking around, and being reckless. They get to the point where they do not care anymore. Deprived of love, emotion, and affection for so long, they step out. Now I understand why he, to this day, will deny or have selective or suppressed memories as if he didn't do certain things. Because although he did, proof and all, that wasn't him. He didn't want to be the person he was with me. I believe he would've never treated her the way he treated me. I saw them interact, and it was beautiful. They had a connection that he and I didn't have. But good ole' religion. (Smile).

In some cases, you should've left a long time ago or allowed it to fall apart naturally when it was falling apart. Then you wouldn't have found yourself in someone else's arms. Maybe you should've left or not begged them to return when they left. Some people that have stepped out have never done anything like this before, and they're just tired. It's no excuse, but it does mean it's time to evaluate your true desires and take steps necessary to manifest them. It also keeps you from hurting others when you honestly and authentically express and pursue your true passions, even if it turns your world upside down. In time things will heal, and all will work out.

Fox and I were like oil and water and still are today. He's pretty much the same person I remember, but I am an entirely different version of who he married. I do not believe Fox intentionally married me wanting to love someone else. He may agree or not, but I did him a favor when I left because I was always meant to be who I am today, and we would not fit. Although it was painful at the time, I freed him to be with his divine partner, whether he is with them or not; he's free. He deserves to be just as happy as I plan to be when I'm boo'd up. I jokingly say the only thing we agree on is how to handle a situation if someone is messing with our kids. We'll be at the school or wherever collaborating in the blink of an eye. And we'll roast each other now and then for a good laugh. But that's it.

FINISH IT

Even my daughter believes that it would be worse if we were still together. She thinks she would be a different person, as well. I agree. She wouldn't be the resilient little firecracker that she is. It's a sobering thought that trying to hold on to things for the wrong reason could be holding up the other party from finding and living their truth in love or any mission in life. If only he and I could've figured this out and known the truth, it would've still ended, but there could've been a more peaceful resolution. We could've avoided so much turmoil and co-parented much more smoothly in the beginning. Lesson learned.

WILL THEY RETURN?

February 2019

"The saying goes, 'I can do bad all by myself,' but sometimes I can do better by myself even if just for a season."

During this three-year journey, I have lost a few close connections. You have heard that you need to heal before the next thing can come into your life. True. But some, including myself during this time, have this hope that if we heal and get better, it will restore the connection. We have this inner hope and lingering thought that maybe after some time, they will come back, and we can reconcile. We try to fix ourselves and the areas we assume made them leave in the first place. **But the key is to heal with no motive.** Attempting to recover to get someone back, is not true healing.

Heal for the sake of healing, and only then you can yield the purest results, whatever they may be. Meaning, whatever is supposed to come to you, whatever is supposed to be, will be in its purest form. I have found that in any relationship if someone is meant to be in your life, there is a flow. There is an ebb, but it flows again. It's not perfect. You teach and learn from each other, grow together. The love deepens. But if you must direct every step and always remind someone of what you need or repeat yourself, it creates tension. That may not be your person. Look at the calm

FINISH IT

waters on a beach. It comes and goes like in relationships. Up and downs. But if the waves are crashing year after year, 24/7, and we find ourselves on the phone telling someone about it, year after year, 24/7, we may need to reconsider some things. I have been a listening ear for so many people, and it is year after year.

Hear this truth. We know that it is not the right person, but we don't want to change, grow, or evolve. We want to save face. If we leave, we would have to explain, expand, not be co-dependent or be alone for a while. So, we stay and complain. At least we have company in our misery, sex now and then and finances can remain intact. We hold on because we're afraid of *becoming*. Becoming who we are meant to be and being with the people that match our energy. It takes courage. We hide in these relationships pointing the finger, playing the victim, and settling. Or we cheat to avoid facing our reality.

Why are you still parenting someone by steadily telling them how to treat you? Is that your person? There were times when we separated during that marriage, well when he kept leaving, and it is always painful for the party who is left behind. Some people do not recommend that. But it is necessary sometimes. During those times, we can grow and transform into the person we need to be, and they need to be, and it can come back together in a healthier form. However, the reality is, some people choose not to grow and change, nor are they meant to if that is not their destiny. In the separation, we see what we need to see. I saw that nothing was changing.

We waste time trying to tell them, transform them, and make them into who we want them to be so that we will feel that we are treated right. We let people turn us into something that we're not. We couple-up with people not aligned with who we desire to be. When I was married, First Lady of a church, with my worship leader self, and even before marriage, I was laid back, chill, quiet, non-violent, and mild. But when things became clear the last year of that marriage, I vaguely remember throwing an iron, cussing, re-enlisting to perform detective work thinking we're past that, etc. When I must become a part-time detective, something is out of alignment, and I ignored that part in the marriage. People would often send me things to investigate because I was so naïve. Why do I have to do this? It was not my character. No, the iron was not hot; it was just the closest thing to me. After years of *allowing* it, I was turning into someone I was not. Out of character behavior is a red flag.

From experience, persistently telling them how they need to treat you, what you want, and need is another major red flag. Your person, though not perfect, instinctively deep down inside will know what you need for the most part. I have experienced both sides of the coin; from lack of time, affection and attention to receiving that 'Good Morning' text, getting a music video sent to me as a song dedication, complimenting me when I looked my worst, getting a poem, etc. And I never asked for that out loud, but in my heart, I secretly desired it. When I did get it if only for a short time, I knew I was not crazy. My desires are real and attainable. The sad part is, it makes both parties look bad when it is as simple as we do not belong together. Because the stuff that a person will not do with you, they will do with another. Then we are shocked or become insecure because of it.

Lastly, hurt people hurt people is a reality but not a justification. We are still responsible for how we treat people. Opportunities are presented to heal those areas so that we can stop hurting people.

Heartbreak

2/04/19 Heartbreak, heartbreak, heartbreak. What a blow. Letting go. I feel like 95% of my life has been nothing but heartbreak. I am numb. I cannot cry today. I have not seen him since we met. Distance, miles, and other priorities on both ends keep us apart. Why did we even meet?

FINISH IT

02/05/19 Today I cried. I wept! I cussed! I wailed! I yelled! I was doing fine for these last several years, and I never asked for love to come into my life, let alone come and leave. Again!

2/06/19 I need to work on the next set of songs, but I am so broken I cannot get up off the floor to reach my laptop or phone. I wish it were just a few feet closer. I am empty. I pray someone, anyone, would text me so I could snap out of this and have a reason to get up. I am so past, asking God why. Almost 40 and that never has been the right question. Trying not to lose my mind or go off. It is best for me to be isolated or I will verbally bleed all over people.

2/16/19 Today, I spoke for the first time in three years in front of a crowd. It was interesting because I left my notes at home on 'accident,' so I just flowed. Most of the people were church people, and I left the church three years ago. As I spoke, I healed. I shared details about my life that I didn't plan to, just like in this freakin' book.

2/19/19 I told my friend that I am amazed that all I have to show after a storm is spiritual growth. Yes, I was venting. Is that the encouragement that I am going to get? "Well, you will be stronger than before?" Yeah, stronger to handle the next painful storm! Can I get something tangible to show for my victory? Like a real long-term relationship, or financial abundance that lasts, or something I've been desiring? I am so tired of coming out of the storm empty-handed or almost getting it. Can your girl win for a change? Geez.

2/20/19 Today was incredibly taxing. I cried all day whenever I was alone. The pain. The hopelessness of losing all hope. I told my friend that if I had to do this life all over again, I wouldn't. I don't like it here. Yes, I am grateful as things could be worse, but the injustice, the pain, the heartache and cycles of storms and rain is just too much at times. And not in my life alone, but those around me. And why did the Universe show me that and I can't have it?! Looking for a breakthrough. I need a breakthrough.

2/20/19 A breakthrough. Later this evening, an unexpected call from a family member I had not spoken to in over a year and a half called to clear the air. I was so overwhelmed, thankful, and happy. I needed that. I have so much respect for her, like more than ever. She has no idea how much it meant to me. The situation is what inspired the song *Love for You* from the album.

MY LIFELINES

"When can I start dating mom?" asked my then 14-year-old. "When Hell freezes over." I mean, "When I start dating." I replied jokingly. That's exactly how it happened. Man, I forget how powerful our words are sometimes. When I started dating or what I thought was dating in 2017, a few months later she came to me about a boy. She was 15 by then. Granted, we made a pact that she could start dating when I did. Here's the kicker. I had no plans to date ever again in this lifetime, so I thought the joke would be on her. Jokes on me!

"It can be a mother's nightmare when her teen daughter comes to her about liking a boy. But it's every mother's dream when she tells you ALL about it."

I mean everything! It was bittersweet. Simultaneously, the protector in me wanted to shield her from the heartache, challenges, and pain that can come when a relationship does not work out. But then I also felt peace and underlying serenity that for the most part, I was the only person she would come to for advice. She asked how to respond to specific texts, and how she felt about showing affection in a relationship and how soon is too soon to kiss. The best way for me to explain the chaos that was going on inside of me was every time she brought up the subject, I was ready to fight somebody, anybody if necessary, anyone nearby. And at the same time, relishing in this beautiful bond that I had with my teenage daughter.

MY LIFELINES

I felt like exploding because I just wanted to protect her, but at the same time *allow* her. My daughter has watched her friends engage in *everything* since the 6th grade. But she stayed focused and waited until she was mature enough even to consider it. I still do not like it because I think she is too young. Give me a second. I need to go to the piano before I throw this laptop just thinking about it! I'm okay. Or am I?! Ugh.

I remember a piece of advice that I gave to her when she was dealing with a challenge. I told her that she needed to continue to develop into the person that she is meant to be so that she can attract the same thing. For me, I found it helpful to make sure that a guy is honestly single if he wants to have anything to do with me. It is not going to work if you are ready for stability, and this person still wants to date multiple people or already in a relationship. You want to find someone who is single-minded like you. I believe that you can manifest and co-create precisely what is in your heart. You do not have to settle, and you do not have to do it the way other people do it or society says you must do it. My daughter is a rare jewel, and I am impressed by her. She is my twin, I know.

Winning with Autism

I will admit it was difficult to accept that my son was autistic, and it's still challenging because of my personality, not his. After all, in 2009, I believed this wasn't supposed to happen to me as an African American and Christian who served God. These are the false assumptions that I had back before the diagnosis. Seriously. Telling this to a black Christian for the most part, resulted in the child doused in holy oil and hours at the altar casting out demons. I have seen it! And black society said that was an issue for "white people." I used to think that, but not anymore. But why did I think that way? Primarily because Caucasians openly spoke about it and took their kids to the doctor for testing. I didn't see any black people

FINISH IT

doing that back then. For one, they could not afford it. Black culture just whipped the kid and or took them to the pastor for prayer.

My son is one of the sweetest, yes ma'am, yes sir, well-mannered, funniest individuals you will ever meet, and he is consistent in his emotions. I need that. He'll send me texts while in class asking me what's wrong with the world mom and why are people so hateful and disrespectful. I put my head down and thought, "I'm sorry son, I'll do better." I'm kidding; he was referring to kids mistreating teachers. He has a big heart. My family noticed his 'special gift' at about ten months. Yeah, he was different, walking around with his one sock. But it was cute to me. I still watch home videos of him in a diaper and one sock. I had to come back to this paragraph on 5/15/19 and guess what? This boy is 14…walking around the house with one sock on right now! Love it. At the age of four, I took him in to see how to nurture his gift and get the tools I needed to make sure he succeeds. And that he has!

He just placed 1st at regionals and 2nd in the state competition for Kickstart and earned the competitor of the year award last week. At the ceremony, the instructor was going on and on about some kid. I was like, "Goodness gracious, geez, who is he talking about?" He called my son's name, and we both were shocked! He wasn't even paying attention, no surprise. I'm scrambling for my phone to capture him receiving his engraved belt with his name on it. My sister was sitting somewhere else and told me later she knew they were talking about him. Big deal? Yes, for a kid who used to ask me why he was different, why does he think this way, who used to self-reject, who tried out for every sport and never made any team and struggled to make friends until this year. His Kickstart teacher called me and said that technically he could compete with the "special needs" division for a guaranteed trophy, but thought he was good enough to compete with the general students even without a guaranteed win. There'd be no special treatment if I agreed to it. He'd have to earn it on his own. I told him since he sees my son every day as his instructor, for him to make that call. He said he believed in him and that my son could handle it. And that he did.

I needed my son during my marriage, the divorce, and to this day. That was such a dark time, and he possessed consistent joy. I am a thinker. Analytical. I am more balanced now, but he used to and still does walk up to my face with a smile and stare at me. (Personal space, bro.) And he may ask me if I'm okay or if my day is going well. It was like looking in a mirror and seeing a serious looking woman overthinking, trying to figure it all out and make things work. He is my chill pill. He brings me balance. He is light-hearted when I get heavy. When I attempt to get on him or fuss about leaving crumbs or something trivial, he comes out, fixes it, and then smiles at me. Geez. Like, it is not that serious Dorian. I made it through my marriage and divorce because of them both. He was a joyful distraction along with his hilarious sister. They are my lifelines.

You Have Two Kids?!

It's hilarious when guys find out that I have two teenagers *and* I am 39. I primarily attract younger guys who assume I am in my early thirties, and some propose late twenties when I tell them to guess. Of course, when my kids were three and four, I was not worried about getting into another relationship and thought like most single mothers, it would be harder to find someone because of the kids. Man, please. Here's what I know. If a man is attracted to me, it is the woman that my kids made me. If it were not for them, I would not be the woman that I am. They have taught me just as much as I have taught them. So how can you want me and not want the product that made me? Fair enough, people have their preferences, and when they were younger, I was not ready for anything or anyone but healing. But now I am all grown, and this triad has

FINISH IT

been standing strong going on ten years, and we are all ready to give and receive love.

Most of the gentlemen callers said that they didn't pick up on me being a mother or older. That's because I'm not a mother or my age first. I am Dorian first. They may have assisted in shaping me, but they do not define me. I feel like I lost my identity in that marriage. But even if you are married, you don't have to let that happen. You are still you. Plus, your spouse and kids will benefit from your self-cultivation.

One thing I've realized is that I was *Dorian* before kids and will be *Dorian* when they leave this house. I focus on cultivating her first, as my other roles are an extension of me, enhanced by my inner work. My kids will tell you. I don't care who wants to go to the movies or get picked up from wherever. If this was my already scheduled sacred time for myself, I'm not leaving this spot. Unless dropping them off gives me more sacred time (smiling). I will always be there for them, no matter what. Let that be known. But it's all about balance, my new word for life. No matter how young your children are, find, and keep your sacred time. Yes, you do have time! And not just time when they are napping. Make and create time. Manifest the money or favor you need to get a good sitter and hit those streets or the bed!

This way, I don't resent my children or blame them for my life being unpleasant, or that I missed out on something or feel obligated to give myself totally to them just because I'm their mother; balance. Again, motherhood is one aspect of me.

LESSONS LEARNED

March 2019

3/08/19 Jim is back for a few days. We laid three more songs down and went to the studio to practice visuals for the music video and stage performance.

3/12/19 Spoke with my make-up artist about the look we are going to go with based on my music. We worked together before when I was creating Christian music, but this is a new genre for me and a new *me* period. He heard a few songs but said as everyone else has, there is something about that song, *Fallen*.

3/15/19 Nothing like a friend who is in tune with you so much so that she will jump in her car as soon as she hears an inkling of a cry and be there ASAP! Thank you, friend. It seems like the hardest day of my life so far this year. I would have broken down right there in that restaurant if she had not of walked me to the parking lot. Then I broke down. At times it seems like a glimpse of something is worse than not ever experiencing it at all.

3/17/19 After four years, I went to church today. I woke up, and before I could open my eyes, I saw a church building in my mind. The day before, I was at the store, and the clerk mentioned that he would be going to church the next day after asking what I was going to do.

FINISH IT

3/20/19 Clearing out. Today I continue to clear out people that do not resonate with my life and close out cycles with them that have nothing to do with my future.

3/21/19 Lots of transitions, transformations, endings and new beginnings this month. Lots of purging and of course, inner healing. A lot of crying!

3/23/19 Reflecting on meeting Twin. He doesn't know that his presence is with me or maybe he does. Even when it comes to dealing with other guys. He set a standard! I was able to block and release someone(s) who only had interest in themselves but wanted me to embrace what they were offering *on their terms*. Baffled at how people think they can just come back and get what they want when it is convenient for them. So proud of myself. I know what I want, and I know my worth. If you are not willing to put in the work, you are not ready or have not earned the payoff. *"You Thought"* on the album was written just for them.

April 2019

4/1/19 I'm glad for a new month with new energy. The month of March was hell for me emotionally.

4/4/19 Well, I decided to release an EP in June instead of a full album that would not be ready until the Fall. It was always my intent to make it available for the summer, but something got lost in translation. One talk with music dad got us on track to make that happen. I cherish him.

4/5/19 My friend made me throw away my Nope hat. We were out eating, and she told me to throw it away and stop putting that energy out into the universe.

Yep. That was the purpose of me buying it primarily to ward off guys in the grocery store or wherever. I bought it in 2017 and wore it proudly. It did the job because whenever I felt them following me down the aisle, I'd turn around with a straight face; "I know you see

LESSONS LEARNED

this hat and this look on my face." It worked every time. That was in my anti-love phase. But I told her it could mean no to the bull crap, or no I won't take this or that, etc. She said, "Well if you say yes to what you want and send that energy out, you won't have to worry about saying no to anything else." I threw it away as soon as I got home. She was right. One older man broke through and asked me what it meant to me and thought it was funny. He wanted one to wear around the house for his three daughters.

4/07/19 Random, but I realized today that control as far as my gifts, money, time, etc. are issues I had with the church and why it's not appealing to me to join one. If people knew my story, they would understand.

Whether I was a member, the music director, or the pastor's wife, I was told where to be, what to wear, and *how* to be; for 20 years, with nothing to show for it. In this new place in my life, I am so free and the idea of being told when to be somewhere and how often is not desirable. Just being transparent. I want to be open to pursue my gifts and share them with the world as I am intuitively guided to do so. Maybe it's me bucking 20 years of being controlled or just my soul's path or both. I'll have to look more into that. People will say, "You do it for your 9-5 job, don't you?" Well, not when you work for yourself and have the freedom to create wealth for yourself. I know that not all places are like this, but that's been my experience.

4/12/19 Headed to Florida, the home of my book publishing company, to meet some people, write, get inspired, and see that beach! Check this out. I have always wanted to go to Florida since I was a teenager with absolutely no reason, connection, or purpose. I know now that I was manifesting that and there were books inside of me that would connect me to Florida. Amazing! We are co-creators!

4/14/19 Are you KIDDING ME?! In the ER the night I get back from Florida.

FINISH IT

4/15/19 Wow. Another connection from the past. Not romantic but a fellow musician. He mentioned how he stood up for me once when I left our church back in the day. In other words, he knew I refused advances and that being one of the reasons I left. He spoke up about it, and they didn't like it. Pretty cool.

4/19/19 In two weeks, Jim will be here for a week, so we can do vocals every day to be ready for the June release. Life is about to change for me, of course in the best way and with that much is required of me. I spend a lot of time contemplating these changes. *I have changed.*

4/21/19 When you know what's coming, you can settle in and get ready for the ride. OH MY! I am going back and editing this book and just noticed that in November I told my mom I hoped the album and book would complete by May, but some setbacks and misunderstandings kept pushing the finish line all the way to Fall. But it's settled. Jim is coming May 4th to finish the album, all on hope.

4/26/19 I cannot even express in words the kind of day this was. I took a huge financial hit that seemingly threatens my personal life, album, book, etc. I'm mortified! How can this happen? All they could do is apologize. On the inside, there is a peace I cannot explain. But outwardly, I could not hold the tears back all day. I hyperventilated a few times or had panic attacks or something.

4/27/19 Meeting with Misty today to go over looks for the book and album! Love her energy and so excited to team up with her. My heart is pleased. All I can do now is create the finances I need and keep moving forward.

4/30/19 I'm closing out this cycle and clearing my energy to prepare for him. All I can do is create the love life, again, that I want and keep moving forward. Brand new start starting tomorrow. I will heal and prepare to receive.

People

I love people! But I have learned people. Still learning. Knowing people will keep you from blaming them for allegedly hurting you. Yes, people do and say things that hurt, but you can handle it better, knowing that it has nothing to do with you when someone treats you that way. Unless you are a butt, and what they do to you is a natural consequence for your behavior. When I take inventory over every time I cried or was in pain over someone else's actions, I find out that there is some other stuff going on in and with them. I've also noticed that some of the hurt I said they caused was already there, and their presence and actions triggered and reminded me of areas in need of healing. I know this is true because now that I've healed abandonment issues, rejection, insecurity, etc. if someone were to walk out of my life, I would have nothing but love for them and keep living. Of course, naturally, those triggers may arise if I have opened my heart to someone. But I will not stay down or cry for long. Am I heartless? No. Whole? Yes. And I realize that some people are for a season or a reason. People have free will, and I know my worth.

***Dorian* is the coolest chic, I know.** Real talk. I love being with her, and she makes me laugh. Who wouldn't want to hang around me? But I understand we all have our journey. This knowledge inspired the song and lyrics for, *Love for You*.

I see people of faith, Christians, borderline hating, yelling, and shaking their heads at people that are hurt, broke, and lost. But if you read your Bible, you would know that Jesus, who is supposed to be the role model for the Christians, only yelled, fussed and got upset with the people that should've known better. But the people of faith are on social media condemning and judging people who need to be loved. Do you think that people are not aware of what they are doing and the choices they are making? Of course, they are, even if they have never read a Bible. We all have an inner knowing or moral compass that was given by the Creator.

Why else would someone cover up a murder weapon or try to hide evidence if there was nothing wrong with their actions? Outside of extreme mental issues, everybody knows what they are doing and pointing it out is not going to fix it. It can make it worse for some. I find that just being me, like Jesus did with Zacchaeus, can inspire someone into wholesome action if that is what is needed. If I recall, he just wanted to see who Jesus was.

There is too much of *Dorian* that needs to be focused on to post and judge someone else's choices. I am amazed at how many perfect people there are out there. Or who negatively comment on someone's page with all these scriptures, as if, judging a person posting a provocative photo is worse than a person who lied to their boss about being sick or not keeping their word about something. The lesson for me is to focus on me and love others unconditionally.

IT'S ALMOST TIME

May 2019

05/01/19 Jim will be here soon for six days to finish the vocals for the debut album. It has been a tough day purging things...healing. I still believe that everything will be okay. I am not surprised.

05/04/19 Jim is here! Six days straight to finish this album! And guess what? I REFUSE to let this Texas weather beat me up. I have suffered from severe allergies since I was a teenager, which makes singing a challenge at times. Of course, they want to act up the final week of recording, but no! I will conquer these vocals. I am going to do just fine. Period. I also know that when you are healing from emotional wounds or spiritually, you purge. And that can result in physical symptoms and the release of things from your body. The physical and spiritual world connect. But really? We want to heal and purge this week? Okay. Okay.

05/05/19 Day 2- Allergies were kicking my butt even harder today than yesterday. I need to see a specialist because this is ridiculous! I can hardly breathe, and it is year-round! Jim keeps recording my snorts and threatening to blackmail me with it (smile). But the vocals are done, and they sound fantastic despite the struggle.

5/6/19 Day 3- Was a bit of a battle today. Always a challenge to connect with a song about heartbreak when you are happy/

FINISH IT

healed again. Music dad set me straight after a whole hour of "I can't" and "I don't" want to go back there.

Music Dad: "It's your job as the artist to go there again. You're holding yourself to a standard of how you sang it when you wrote it, but you're not there anymore. Instead of singing it from a place of pain and frustration, sing it from a place of empowerment!"- Jim Finley. And there it is.

5/9/19 Day 6-Here we go again. Another sad love song that I do not want to sing. It is the last day of recording the vocals, and I am not feeling it. Music dad gave me some stern looks and refused to let me walk out and quit. He told me that this is usually the part of the process when songs do not make it on the album. I had to push and visit that emotional place again or else. It is the one song that could be the most successful, and what if I don't record it? But I did. I did.

5/12/19 Overwhelmed. I cannot take this anymore. I have these projects that need funding, and this big financial hit?! Now?! I feel like I am about to break. I cannot even speak. My chest hurts. All I can do at this point is believe. My joy is gone, and I want to walk off into the woods and never return! But I can't. I have come too far. Unbelievable, but I will have to believe. It always works out.

5/17/19 Well, this may be the last journal entry I write before this baby goes off to print. Unless I need to and can slip another one in during the final approval process. What a journey. I can take a breath. I will see you guys on the other side. Hugs and kisses for any support today and in the future. I love you all, and I'm glad to be on this journey together with you.

5/30/19 I get to slip this in. I am cuddled up on the floor in a corner of blankets, pillows, and snacks. My daughter just came in and saw me going through almost 50,000 words in my manuscript for this book, for the 5th time! She hands me a bottle of water and

IT'S ALMOST TIME

says, "Mom, I am so proud of you, doin' your thing. Now get back at it." Can you say, worth it?!

June 2019

Yay! I have a little more time to write while we wait for the photoshoot. June is the final month to get er' done. I am excited, uneasy, at peace, in awe, but it's all coming together. The book and album are complete now; we only need the pictures. My stylist has worked overtime to get the looks together for my events and the projects. This month I have my first full public music performance and a play that I will perform in, as myself, *DorianMarie*. June 13th, Jim calls. "How does it feel to have your EP in your hands?" Now *that* was a conversation. I finished it, and it will be released this time. Overwhelmed is an understatement. My dream is and has come true. What the heck?! Of course, music dad was in full effect on that call, with encouraging words, how proud he was, and I am not going to cry. But he also came as a friend who wants me to win. We recalled the first time he came and recorded these songs in my house in an empty room, amazed at how it all came together. We did it!

The event on June 15th, where I did ten cover songs, was a success! I loved that show as it set the tone for *DorianMarie*. Oh yes, from the songs chosen for me to my wardrobe. My stylist strategically chose the outfit, and I owned it! That is who I am though shocking to some. And this photoshoot? It was flawless! Everyone was there. Jim almost didn't make it, but I got a text that said, "Music dad will be in the building." YES!! We'd come so far, and his presence along with the whole team sealed it all. My photographer was phenomenal, unique, and energetic. If you only knew the setbacks that I have faced and now face. But I can't say it enough; it is still coming together. I finished it in the face of adversity.

FINISH IT

After the shoot, I had an interview, where I spoke about the book and the album. That was a long but productive day. My baby girl was right there assisting everyone. Once the interview was done, so were we. Man, I appreciate every positive comment, like, share and shout out on social media and personal texts from my friends and supporters. I see you. You've been receptive of my transformation, and I'm taking it all in.

I look forward to growing in my connection with you all as I create content that will inspire, heal, and propel you into wholesome action. I thank you for streaming/downloading *"My Other Playlist"* as well as getting a copy of this book. Thank you.

6/28/19 Album is available! And guess who just inboxed me a message? Pierre, after seven years!!

The most valuable lesson that I've learned is that just as I promote allowing others to be who they are, with boundaries, I finally allowed *Dorian* to do what she felt was best for her. It's my favorite part of the book writing about allowing myself, showing compassion to myself, mercy and grace to myself, being tender with myself...everything that I've been to others my whole life. It's the first time I've ever treated myself this way completely.

I've also learned that I don't have to go, be, or stay in a situation that no longer serves me or fits the path I am led to take. Man, this was a problem for me. It stemmed from my first heartbreak. When someone cheats on you, insecurity will set in making you feel like you are not good enough, unworthy and something is wrong with you. So, from then on, I accepted any relationship as it was. In my mind, I didn't deserve any better. Because if things were right with me, he would have never cheated, right? If there was abuse, I deserved it. So, I moved on to the next one, with more abuse, cheating, etc. Yep, something is wrong with me, I thought. It's all that comes to me, so it is meant to be. They always have another option, and the choice is never me. I felt powerless! What astounds me, is that they all came back even up to this January, saying that it was their fault, young age, peer pressure, immaturity and that I was perfect. And all these years, I blamed myself.

I did play the role of an empath. I attracted broken people in need of healing. I had a form of brokenness too, always ready to mend and remedy their pain, to my demise. I was also attracting the same type of guy so that I could finally heal that subconscious part of me that says, "That is all you will ever get and deserve."

We need to heal before quickly moving on to the next relationship, to prevent recreating the same story with a different person. I don't care what anyone says. I shouldn't have stayed in that marriage that long or married that person, to start. I shouldn't have stayed in that church for that long. And I should be singing the music I want to. But I had to learn the lessons. We only have one life, and no one knows what goes on behind closed doors as you do. And no one knows the effort you have put in to make things work in your relationships and even on jobs. Same applies to places of employment. If you complain every day, either you are ungrateful, need to find another spot, or you need to go in faithfully with the right attitude while you work on building your dream career or job off the clock. This way, you can wake up happy no matter what you do or where you work.

IN CONCLUSION

Well, here is where I end this family. Will I get blocked or unfriended by those who knew me back then? Maybe. Will I get called a heretic, or one of the "elect" that has fallen away? Maybe. Will I be put on the prayer list and unfollowed? Maybe. I may never sing on some church stages after this. But will I continue to love people, live in peace with my new-found freedom and in the comfort of my own skin? Fasho! That means for sure.

My story does not have to be your truth, so make your choices in love, music, and faith according to your convictions and what resonates with you.

FINISH IT

Cliché to hear that when your plans fall through, know that there are bigger plans for you. Well, the first time I around I begged, pleaded and I planned to put out music for the church. And I know that people are thinking that, "She used to make music for the church, but now she is making music for the *world*," referring to sinners, you know, worldly people or fallen saints. But I am not making music for the church or the world only. I am making music for the entire *Universe*!

THE ALBUM

This album honors the part of me that I didn't honor for years, at least publicly. At home, I would crank up all kinds of music and dance in ways that were not suitable for a church stage. I don't mean derogatory, just whatever my body wanted to do naturally. If I didn't say, I was a fitness instructor, so dancing, moving, and choreography was a part of that. I didn't see how it fit into my faith walk. I felt conflicted behind what the church would think, so I decided to find some Christian work out videos to avoid hell (smile). Honestly, that was boring because I wanted to move! I love to work out, dance, and I love being in love. It seems like pain comes with all of those. That is what this album is about, the highs and lows of being in love.

I find it surprising and ironic that I am on this new path, creating songs that promote love, unity, and relationships of all types and especially romantic relationships. Below I will explain each song and include the lyrics. While written in real time, the album and the book intend to be released together or around the same time. So, depending on the printing process and completion of everything, I may switch up lyrics in case you hear some variations. I wrote all of these between September 2018 and January 2019, and there is a person(s) tied to each song.

FINISH IT

My Other Playlist – The Album

Love for You

*This was the first record I wrote for the album. I have lost and regained a few close relationships out of the blue with no explanation. Even if there is no reconciliation, there is nothing but love here. Some connections are not meant to come back together, and I am okay with that because that is how it is intended to be for all our highest good.

I was alone last night thinkin' about all of my relational losses
Like my best friend my best man even my kin
Dropped off like we never happened
So unexpected is this rejection or is there a greater cause
I may never know why you had to go, but one thing is for sure
There's something that I want to tell you
I really want you to know
I've got nothing in my heart but love for you

Now let's be clear this didn't happen overnight; It took some time
To process my feelings, endure the healing, try to figure out why
Promised forever nothing could sever you from my life
Well I may never know why you had to go, but one thing is for sure
Maybe in another life, maybe in another time
We'll find our way, back to each other
Someday, we'll find our way back to each other

Was It A Mistake?

*This was the second record for the album. It talks about a connection I had during this process. I had not heard from this person in a while. I was ghosted on and off. Sometimes we are more vested in a relationship than the other

THE ALBUM

person and are then forced to look in the mirror, learn the lesson, and rebuild our faith in our decision making and discernment process. I thought if this is not it, and I had all of these so-called signs and feelings, I cannot trust my intuition or heart or even God to lead me. I know I prayed, but it still didn't come together. I mislead myself...again

Was it a mistake, if the choice I made, made me a better me
Is it fair to blame or call names for the pain that I didn't see
You were just a mirror, and you made it clearer
That I'm not where I thought I should be

I'm thinking of the day, I took your hand, I thought you had mine
Now I'm all alone, in my feelings, dear God what went wrong
Is this another test, that I'm failing or a game I am forced to play

Was it a Mistake, cause' if I'm wrong how can I
Ever trust in this heart again

Was it a mistake, if in choosing you, I discovered me
Everything has changed, I'm not the same, I'm more of who I want to be
And I'm still alone, but I'm healing
This time apart, is what we needed, I needed

I'm goin' round and round tryna to figure out
How you've opened my heart but you're not around
This love felt so real
There's one more thing I need to ask you
One thing I need to know

If I'm wrong how can I, ever trust in love, again

FINISH IT

Tell Me

*So, I believe that people can send you messages telepathically and that we are connected spiritually. We receive messages in our dreams. Sometimes people have a hard time getting these messages in real life because of anxious minds. When you go to sleep, you'll get your answers if you set that intention. What's interesting is that I haven't dreamed about this person in weeks, maybe even a month or so. And lo and behold, last night I dreamed about him, and the song was incomplete. But when I woke up, I had the vamp, and I wrote it based on what happened in the dream. I wake up with a song every morning, and I know it is a message for me.

You invade my dream space
You're telling me the things that you should have said to my face
Your energy hounds me
I'm waking up to lyrics that you should have sung to me
Withholding your emotion, tryna to keep me under your potion
I know that it's a mask, so baby why you holding back

You say you have no feelings, but you can't stay away
I ask you if you want me, but you have nothing to say so

Tell me, tell me that you want me, you want me
You need me, you want me, you love me

I can feel your longing
Desire so strong I don't know how long I
Can watch your replays
You're claiming my heart but stuck in your thoughts
Withholding your emotion, tryna keep me under your potion
I know that it's a mask, so baby why you holding back

I don't know how you feel is it pretend, or it's real

THE ALBUM

But I don't want to waste another day of my life
Tryna figure out if you want to be in mine
So, I'm closing the door no more tears on the floor
I'm free and open now to find the love of my life
Find the one with a heart like mine

Fallen

After being closed for years, I decided to open my heart for the first time. I was open to it, but he was not ready for that. There was a lot of ghosting, in and out energy on their part while I fell all by myself.

I took the fall, when I took a chance, on a love that could never stay still
You overtook, I over gave, like a game you ran I chased
Though we made each other better, we could never come together
Why were you so afraid?
Tried to show you I was different, but your mind was always split and
For you, a choice was never made

But I chose to fall in love, with you baby
Hoping to fall in your arms
I chose to fall in love, know it sounds crazy
But I'm willing to risk it all and fall for you
Fallen

I took the fall, when I gave my all, not knowing where this thing would go
You led me on, and I went along, I can see we both were wrong
Though we made each other better, we could never come together

FINISH IT

Why were you so afraid?
Tried to show you I was different, but your mind was
always split and
For you, a choice was never made

Let's fall together, and stand in this love forever
Let's fall and let go, and hold on to this love forever

Lifetime

My encounter with Twin inspired this song. No explanation needed, just pure bliss.

I can see it in your eyes, caught us by surprise, unexpected love
An unusual connection, beyond understanding, an amazing love

There's nothing about you; I can't see myself
Living the rest of my lifetime with
You are the one, and it's a perfect fit, hey
There's nothing about you, I can't see myself
Living the rest of my lifetime with, no, oh, oh, oh

Will we share love in this lifetime, or will we just let it
pass us by?
Don't let it pass us by baby

I can feel it in your touch, never felt so much, it's more
than chemistry
We were made for each other, more than lifetime lovers
You're my destiny, boy you are my destiny

I like your lips, I like your nose, I like your hips, I like your toes
That's what he told me

THE ALBUM

You Thought

The Single! It's self-explanatory, but after a conversation with an ex, I got off the phone disturbed. So, I wrote about it. It was initially about one person, but another one came back with the same energy. So, it is about two people.

You thought you could come back around, and everything would fall in place
A happy ever after, well baby that's not the case
See I was done and over the day you showed me
That I was not enough
I was just a young girl, and so in love

You thought you thought
You thought that I would wait
And you'd come back, you could come back, and I would save your place

You wanted me to reminisce about the good times that we had
But all that I remember is the reason that I left
See I was done and over the day I woke up alone in my own dreams
I know that I'm enough and I can't see you with me

You say that you love me and that it's meant to be
When I was crying my eyes out, you were nowhere to be found
I'm better now; it's amazing how
How you think you deserve, to be in my world, I forgive you
But I don't need you, boy!